WHAT IS THE BOOK OF JEREMIAH?

Kids' Guides to God's Word Series

What Is the Book of Genesis?
What Is the Book of Exodus?
What Is the Book of Leviticus?
What Is the Book of Numbers?
What Is the Book of Deuteronomy?
What Is the Book of Joshua?
What Is the Book of Judges?
What Is the Book of Ruth?
What Is the Book of 1 Samuel?
What Is the Book of 2 Samuel?
What Is the Book of 1 Kings?
What Is the Book of 2 Kings?
What Are the Books of 1–2 Chronicles?
What Are the Books of Ezra & Nehemiah?
What Is the Book of Esther?
What Is the Book of Job?
What Is the Book of Psalms?
What Is the Book of Proverbs?
What Is the Book of Ecclesiastes?
What Are the Books of Song of Songs & Lamentations?
What Is the Book of Isaiah?
What Is the Book of Jeremiah?
What Is the Book of Ezekiel?
What Is the Book of Daniel?
What Are the Books of Hosea–Micah?
What Are the Books of Nahum–Malachi?

What Is the Gospel of Matthew?
What Is the Gospel of Mark?
What Is the Gospel of Luke?
What Is the Gospel of John?
What Is the Book of Acts?
What Is the Book of Romans?
What Is the Book of 1 Corinthians?
What Is the Book of 2 Corinthians?
What Is the Book of Galatians?
What Is the Book of Ephesians?
What Is the Book of Philippians?
What Are the Books of Colossians & Philemon?
What Are the Books of 1–2 Thessalonians?
What Are the Books of 1–2 Timothy & Titus?
What Is the Book of Hebrews?
What Is the Book of James?
What Are the Books of 1–2 Peter & Jude?
What Are the Books of 1-3 John?
What Is the Book of Revelation?

What Is the Book of

JEREMIAH?

Michael Whitworth

ISBN 978-1-971767-29-1

Published by Start2Finish
Bend, Oregon 97702
start2finish.org

Printed in the United States of America

30 29 28 27 26   1 2 3 4 5

CONTENTS

INTRODUCTION

Have you ever tried to warn someone about something and they just wouldn't listen? Maybe you saw a friend heading for trouble and said something, and they blew you off. Maybe you tried again a week later, and they rolled their eyes. Maybe you tried a third time, and they told you to mind your own business. And then the thing you warned them about actually happened, and you stood there watching, feeling helpless and heartbroken, wishing they had listened when there was still time.

Now imagine doing that for forty years. Imagine spending your entire life delivering a warning that an entire nation refuses to hear. Imagine weeping over people who mock you, being thrown into prison for telling the truth, and watching everything you predicted come crashing down in fire and blood and exile.

That's the book of Jeremiah. It's the longest book in the Bible. It's one of the most emotionally raw. And it contains some of the most important promises God has ever made, buried inside some of the most devastating chapters you'll ever read.

WHERE WE ARE IN THE STORY

To understand Jeremiah, you need to know what happened before him. God had chosen Abraham and promised to build a great nation through him. That nation, Israel, grew in Egypt, was rescued in the exodus, received God's law at Mount Sinai, and eventually settled in the land God had promised. Under David and Solomon, the kingdom reached its peak.

Then everything started to fall apart. After Solomon, the kingdom split in two: Israel in the north and Judah in the south. The northern kingdom spiraled into idolatry and was destroyed by Assyria in 722 BC. Gone. Wiped off the map.

The southern kingdom, Judah, survived a little longer. A few good kings, like Hezekiah and Josiah, tried to lead the people back to God. But the overall direction was downhill. The people worshiped foreign gods. The leaders exploited the poor. The prophets told everyone what they wanted to hear instead of what they needed to hear. The temple became a lucky charm rather than a place of genuine worship. And the covenant God had made with his people at Sinai was shattered beyond recognition.

Jeremiah was born into this world around 650 BC, into a priestly family in the small village of Anathoth, just a few miles from Jerusalem. God called him as a young man, possibly still a teenager, and told him his job would be "to uproot and tear down, to destroy and overthrow, to build and to plant." Four of those six tasks are destructive. That should tell you something about the kind of ministry that lay ahead.

Jeremiah would preach through the reigns of five kings, spanning roughly four decades of Judah's final slide toward catastrophe. He would watch the Babylonian empire rise under

Nebuchadnezzar, watch his own people make one suicidal decision after another, and watch the city of Jerusalem burn to the ground in 587 BC. He would be beaten, imprisoned, thrown into a pit, and dragged to Egypt against his will. He would never marry, never have children, and die in a foreign land among people who still refused to listen.

He is called the weeping prophet. After reading his book, you'll understand why.

WHY THIS BOOK MATTERS

Jeremiah matters because it shows us what happens when a nation that knows God refuses to act like it. The people of Judah had the temple, the law, the covenant, and the promises made to David. They had every spiritual advantage imaginable. And they threw it all away, not in a single dramatic moment of rebellion, but in a long, slow drift of comfortable disobedience and willful deafness to God's voice.

That pattern hasn't gone away. The book of Jeremiah is a mirror held up to any community that claims to belong to God but lives as though he doesn't matter.

But Jeremiah also matters because right in the middle of all that darkness, God makes one of the most staggering promises in the entire Bible. He promises a new covenant. Not a patched-up version of the old one that the people kept breaking, but something genuinely new: a covenant written not on stone tablets but on human hearts. A covenant where God himself would fix what was broken inside his people, giving them the ability to know him and obey him from the inside out. A covenant sealed with permanent, total forgiveness.

When Jesus held up a cup of wine at the Last Supper and said, "This cup is the new covenant in my blood," he was pointing straight back to Jeremiah 31. The promise that Jeremiah made to a shattered nation in exile is the promise that Jesus fulfilled on the cross.

WHAT YOU'RE ABOUT TO READ

The book of Jeremiah is long, and it isn't arranged in chronological order. The editors who compiled it organized it by theme and theology, not by timeline. That can feel disorienting, but each chapter of this book will guide you through it in a way that makes sense.

Here's where we're headed:

Chapter 1 covers Jeremiah's call as a young man and the visions that launched his ministry.

Chapter 2 walks through the early poetry of chapters 2–6, where God lays out his case against a people who traded the living God for worthless substitutes.

Chapter 3 covers the temple sermon, where Jeremiah stood in the busiest entrance of God's house and told the people their worship was a lie.

Chapter 4 takes us into Jeremiah's most personal struggles, where we hear his raw, honest, sometimes shocking conversations with God.

Chapter 5 confronts the kings and false prophets who led the nation to ruin, along with the famous letter to the exiles.

Chapter 6 opens the "Book of Consolation," the four-chapter burst of hope containing the new covenant promise and the audacious act of buying a field during a siege.

Chapter 7 tells the story of Jerusalem's fall, including a scroll burned by a king, a prophet rescued from a pit by a foreign official, and the day the walls finally broke.

Chapter 8 follows the survivors into Egypt, where they make one last, fatal choice to reject God's word.

And Chapter 9 sweeps across the nations to show that the God of Israel is the God of the whole earth, before closing the book with a tiny, quiet act of grace in a Babylonian prison.

BEFORE YOU BEGIN

Jeremiah is not easy reading. The grief is relentless. The judgment is severe. A prophet curses the day he was born. Children are sacrificed to pagan gods. A city starves under siege. People who could have been saved refuse, over and over, to listen.

But God doesn't shield us from hard things in Scripture, because hard things are where the deepest truths live. The book of Jeremiah shows us how serious sin really is. It shows us what it costs God to judge the people he loves. It shows us what faithfulness looks like when it doesn't pay off in this lifetime. And it shows us that even at the very bottom, when every human structure has crumbled and every earthly hope has been extinguished, the grace of God is still there, offering a future and a hope to anyone willing to receive it.

The God who speaks in Jeremiah is the same God who sent his Son. The broken covenant that fills these pages is the reason the new covenant was needed. And the tears that Jeremiah shed for his people are the same tears that Jesus would shed over Jerusalem six centuries later, standing on the same hills, loving the same stubborn city, saying, "If only you had known what would bring you peace."

So give this book your attention. It will challenge you. It will break your heart in places. But it will also show you a God whose love is more stubborn than human sin, whose plans outlast every empire, and whose final word is never judgment.

It is always grace.

Turn the page.

1

THE CALL

Have you ever been picked for something you were absolutely sure you couldn't do? Maybe a teacher volunteered you to give a speech in front of the whole school, and your stomach dropped through the floor. Maybe a coach put you in the game at the worst possible moment, and you thought, *There has to be someone better for this.* Maybe someone handed you a responsibility that felt ten sizes too big for you, and all you could think was, *You've got the wrong person.*

Now imagine God shows up and says, "I need you to stand in front of an entire nation and tell them everything they don't want to hear. Kings will hate you. Priests will plot against you. Your neighbors will turn on you. You'll do this for forty years, and almost no one will listen."

That's what happened to Jeremiah. He was young, possibly a teenager, living in a small village outside Jerusalem. He had no political connections, no public speaking experience, and no desire to become the most unpopular person in the country. But God had other plans. And those plans had been in motion before Jeremiah ever took his first breath.

A PRIEST'S SON FROM A SMALL TOWN

The book of Jeremiah opens with a few lines that are easy to rush past, but they set the stage for everything that follows. Jeremiah was the son of a priest named Hilkiah, and he lived in a village called Anathoth, about three miles northeast of Jerusalem. Close enough to see the walls of the capital city. Far enough away to be an outsider.

Anathoth had a history. Centuries earlier, a priest named Abiathar had been banished there by King Solomon after backing the wrong side in a power struggle. The village became home to a priestly family that had been pushed out of Jerusalem's inner circle. If Jeremiah was descended from that family, he would have grown up knowing what it felt like to be on the outside looking in. He would have been well educated in Israel's traditions, steeped in the stories of Moses and the covenant, but removed from the religious establishment that ran things in the capital.

That background matters. God was about to call a prophet who would spend his entire career confronting the people in power. It helps to know that Jeremiah didn't grow up in the palace or the temple. He came from the margins. God has a habit of calling people from unexpected places.

The introduction also names three kings: Josiah, Jehoiakim, and Zedekiah. That single detail tells you that Jeremiah's ministry spanned roughly forty years, from about 627 to 587 BC. Josiah was the best king Judah had seen in generations, a genuine reformer who tried to lead the nation back to God. Jehoiakim was the opposite, an arrogant and oppressive ruler who treated God's word with contempt. Zedekiah was weak and indecisive, a puppet king who couldn't stand up to anyone, including the Babylonian Empire bearing down on his nation.

Jeremiah would have to confront all of them. He was called to speak God's truth to the powerful, and the powerful would fight him every step of the way.

But the most important detail in the introduction isn't about Jeremiah's family or the kings. It's the phrase "the word of the Lord came to him." The book you're about to read isn't a biography. It's not a history textbook. It's the record of what God said through one man over four decades. The words were Jeremiah's. The message was God's. And the two were so intertwined that you can barely tell where one ends and the other begins.

One more thing. The introduction ends with a devastating line: "when the people of Jerusalem went into exile." Before you've even started reading, you know how the story ends. Jerusalem will fall. The temple will be destroyed. The people will be dragged away to Babylon. Everything Jeremiah warns about will come true. You already know the ending. The question is whether anyone will listen before it's too late.

BEFORE YOU WERE BORN

Then comes the moment that changed Jeremiah's life. God spoke to him directly, and the first thing he said was staggering: "Before I formed you in the womb I knew you, before you were born I set you apart; I appointed you as a prophet to the nations."

Read that slowly. Before Jeremiah was born, before he was even fully formed, God already knew him. Not just knew about him the way you might know facts about a stranger. Knew him the way you know your closest friend. The word carries the weight of personal, intimate commitment. God had chosen Jeremiah, singled him out, entered into a relationship with him before he ever drew his first breath.

And God had set him apart. That phrase means something was taken out of the ordinary and reserved for a specific purpose, like a tool placed on a special shelf because it's meant for one particular job. Jeremiah wasn't set apart because he was impressive. He was set apart because God had a mission for him.

That mission? Prophet to the nations. Not just to Judah. Not just to Jerusalem. To the nations. God's concern wasn't limited to one small country in the ancient world. His purposes extended to every kingdom on earth, and Jeremiah would be the one to announce those purposes. This priestly kid from a tiny village was being given a role on the world stage.

"I'M JUST A KID"

Jeremiah's response was about as honest as it gets: "Ah, Sovereign Lord! I do not know how to speak; I am only a child."

We don't know exactly how old he was. The word translated "child" covers everything from a young boy to a teenager to a young man. He was probably somewhere in his late teens. But his point wasn't really about his age. It was about his ability. He didn't have the training, the experience, or the confidence to stand before kings and nations and deliver messages from God. He was a nobody from a small town, and he knew it.

This is one of those moments in the Bible where a pattern shows up. Moses said almost the same thing at the burning bush: "I am slow of speech." Isaiah, when he saw God's glory in the temple, cried out, "I am a man of unclean lips." When God calls someone to a massive task, that person almost always feels completely inadequate for the job. The people who think they're ready for the job are usually the ones God doesn't pick.

But God didn't let Jeremiah off the hook. He didn't argue about whether Jeremiah's concerns were valid. He didn't say, "You're better than you think." He simply overruled the objection: "Do not say, 'I am only a child.' You must go to everyone I send you to and say whatever I command you. Do not be afraid of them, for I am with you and will rescue you."

Two things stand out here. First, Jeremiah would have no choice of audience and no choice of message. He couldn't pick the crowds that would be friendly. He couldn't soften the message to make it more popular. He would go where God sent him and say what God told him to say. Period.

Second, God gave him the one thing that would sustain him through forty years of rejection: "I am with you." Not "You'll be fine." Not "It won't be that bad." Just: I am with you. The same promise God made to Moses, to Joshua, to every servant he ever sent into difficult situations. God's presence doesn't remove the danger. It transforms the person walking into it.

Then God reached out his hand and touched Jeremiah's mouth. "I have put my words in your mouth," he said. The gesture echoed a promise God had made centuries earlier, that he would raise up a prophet like Moses and put his words in that prophet's mouth. Jeremiah was stepping into a role that God had been planning for a very long time.

UPROOT, TEAR DOWN, BUILD, PLANT

God's next words defined what Jeremiah's ministry would

look like: "See, today I appoint you over nations and kingdoms to uproot and tear down, to destroy and overthrow, to build and to plant."

Six verbs. Four of them are about destruction. Only two are about *construction*. That ratio tells you something about the kind of work Jeremiah was being called to do. Most of his career would be spent delivering hard messages, tearing down false confidence, exposing lies, and announcing judgment. The nation had built its life on foundations that couldn't hold. Before anything new could be planted, the old rot had to be pulled out.

But those last two words matter more than you might think. *Build. Plant.* Even in a ministry defined by judgment, God's final intention was restoration. He doesn't tear things down because he enjoys destruction. He tears things down so that something better can grow in the rubble. The four negative verbs describe what had to happen first. The two positive verbs describe where God was heading all along.

For the people who would eventually read this book in exile, sitting in Babylon surrounded by the ashes of everything they'd known, those two words were a lifeline. The uprooting and tearing down had already happened. But building and planting were still ahead.

TWO VISIONS

God confirmed Jeremiah's calling with two visions, each built around something ordinary.

In the first, God asked, "What do you see, Jeremiah?" The prophet answered, "I see the branch of an almond tree."

The almond tree was the first tree to bloom in spring. In the area around Anathoth, almond trees still grow in abundance. When you saw almond blossoms, you knew winter was ending and new life was on its way.

God used the image to make a promise: "I am watching to see that my word is fulfilled." In the original language, the word for "almond" sounds almost identical to the word for "watching." God was making a connection: just as the almond tree is the first to wake up after winter, God is always awake, always watching, always making sure his word comes true. Every time Jeremiah saw an almond tree in bloom, he would remember: God keeps his promises. What he says, he does.

The second vision was darker. "What do you see?" God asked again. Jeremiah answered, "I see a boiling pot, tilting away from the north." Picture a large cooking pot set over a fire, the flames fanned by wind until the water roils and churns. The pot tips, and its scalding contents pour southward.

God's interpretation was blunt: "From the north disaster will be poured out on all who live in the land." Foreign armies were coming. They would pour down from the north like boiling water, overwhelming Jerusalem and all of Judah. Their kings would set up their thrones at the very gates of Jerusalem, a symbol of total conquest and humiliation.

And the reason? "Because of their wickedness in forsaking me, in burning incense to other gods and in worshiping what their hands have made." God's people had broken the most basic commitment of their covenant with him. They had traded the living God for idols they had built with their own hands. They had looked at the God who rescued them from Egypt, who parted the sea, who fed them in the wilderness, and said, "We'd rather worship something we made ourselves."

That betrayal had consequences. The boiling pot was coming.

A FORTIFIED CITY

The chapter ends with God preparing Jeremiah for what lay ahead. And God did not sugarcoat it.

"Get yourself ready! Stand up and say to them whatever I command you." The phrase "get yourself ready" literally means to tighten your belt and prepare for hard work, the kind of language you'd use before going into battle. God wasn't sending Jeremiah on a comfortable assignment. He was sending him into a war.

Then came a warning that should have made Jeremiah's blood run cold: "Do not be terrified by them, or I will terrify you before them." In other words, if Jeremiah let fear of the crowd paralyze him, God himself would become the one he should fear. The only thing more dangerous than facing an angry mob with God's message was refusing to face them at all.

But alongside the warning came a promise, and it was extraordinary: "Today I have made you a fortified city, an iron pillar and a bronze wall to stand against the whole land." God listed Jeremiah's opponents: the kings of Judah, the government officials, the priests, and the ordinary people. Everyone. The entire nation would be against him.

And yet he would not fall. He would be stronger than a walled city, more durable than iron, more resistant than bronze. Not because of his own toughness, but because God would make him that way.

"They will fight against you but will not overcome you, for I am with you and will rescue you."

Here's the remarkable thing: when you read the rest of Jeremiah's story, that promise turns out to be an understatement. Jeremiah was beaten, arrested, thrown into a cistern, and threatened with death more times than you can count. He watched Jerusalem fall. He saw the temple burn. He was dragged to Egypt against his will. But he was never silenced. He was never destroyed. He outlasted the walls of Jerusalem itself. The fortified city crumbled. The iron pillar didn't.

WHAT THIS MEANS FOR US

First, God's plans for you started before you did. Jeremiah was known, chosen, and set apart before he was born. That doesn't mean every detail of his life was locked in from the beginning. It means God had a purpose for him that predated him. The same God who formed Jeremiah in the womb is the God who formed you. You are not an accident. You are not an afterthought. Before you ever knew God, he already knew you.

Second, feeling unqualified doesn't disqualify you. Jeremiah's objection was honest, and God didn't shame him for it. But God also didn't accept it as a reason to find someone else. God's calling doesn't depend on your confidence. It depends on his presence. "I am with you" has always been enough, even when it doesn't feel like it.

Third, God's word will always be fulfilled. The vision of the almond tree was a promise: God is awake and watching. What he says will happen. His promises of grace are as certain as his warnings of judgment. You can count on both.

Fourth, sometimes things have to be torn down before they can be built up. Jeremiah's ministry was defined by four words of destruction and two of construction. That's hard. Nobody wants to hear bad news. But sometimes the lies we believe, the false foundations we've built our lives on, have to be exposed and removed before God can plant something true in their place. If God is tearing something down in your life, it might be because he's making room to build.

Fifth, faithfulness matters more than popularity. Jeremiah was told from day one that everyone would be against him. He would never be popular. He would never see a crowd cheering for his message. But God promised that he would stand. Sometimes doing the right thing means standing alone. If God is with you, that's enough.

TALKING POINTS

1. **God told Jeremiah, "Before I formed you in the womb I knew you."** What does it mean to be known by God before you're even born? How does that change the way you think about your own life and identity?

2. **Jeremiah said he was too young and didn't know how to speak. God didn't deny those things; he just said they didn't matter.** Why do you think God so often chooses people who feel unqualified? What does that tell us about where real strength comes from?

3. **Four of the six verbs in Jeremiah's job description were about tearing down, and only two were about building up.** Why do you think the hard work of removing what's wrong

has to come before the good work of building what's right? Can you think of an example from your own life?

4. **God promised to be with Jeremiah and rescue him, but he never promised that the job would be easy or safe.** What's the difference between God promising to be with you and God promising that nothing bad will happen to you? Which promise matters more, and why?

5. **God warned Jeremiah that the kings, officials, priests, and ordinary people would all fight against him.** If you knew ahead of time that doing the right thing would make you unpopular with almost everyone, would you still do it? What would help you keep going?

Jeremiah had his calling. He had God's words in his mouth and God's promise at his back. But the nation he was sent to didn't want to hear what God had to say. They had abandoned the God who loved them and chased after idols made of wood and stone. And the prophet who had been appointed to confront them was about to find out just how deep the betrayal ran.

Turn the page.

2

THE BETRAYAL

In the movie *Coraline*, a bored girl discovers a secret door in her new house that leads to a parallel world. On the other side is the "Other Mother," who looks like Coraline's real mom but better. The food is incredible. The garden is magical. Everything Coraline ever wanted is right there, handed to her on a silver platter.

There's just one catch. To stay, she has to let the Other Mother sew buttons over her eyes.

The more time Coraline spends in the other world, the more she realizes that nothing there is real. The dazzling food, the beautiful garden, the smiling faces are all a trap designed to lure her in and consume her. The Other Mother doesn't love Coraline. She wants to own her. And the children who came before Coraline, the ones who said yes to the buttons? They're trapped behind a mirror, their souls drained away, with nothing left but ghostly whispers.

Coraline's real mother isn't perfect. The real world isn't as flashy. But it's real. And real love, even imperfect love, is worth more than the most dazzling counterfeit.

That story is a nearly perfect picture of what God describes in Jeremiah 2–6. His people had a relationship with the living God, the one who rescued them from Egypt, fed them in the wilderness, and gave them a land overflowing with good things. He loved them with the kind of love that doesn't quit. And they walked away from all of it to chase after gods that glittered on the surface but had nothing underneath. Gods that promised everything and delivered nothing. Gods that would, in the end, consume them.

These five chapters are some of the most emotionally intense passages in the entire Bible. God isn't just issuing legal charges. He's pouring out the pain of someone who has been betrayed by the person he loves most.

THE HONEYMOON

God opens with a memory. He tells Jeremiah to go to Jerusalem and deliver this message: "I remember the devotion of your youth, how as a bride you loved me and followed me through the desert, through a land not sown."

Picture that. God is looking back at the early days of his relationship with Israel the way someone looks through old photographs. He remembers the wilderness, right after the exodus from Egypt, when the nation was young and dependent and willing to follow him anywhere. They didn't know where they were going. The desert had no food, no water, no safety. But they trusted God enough to follow him into it.

God calls that time a honeymoon. Israel was like a young bride, deeply devoted to her husband. She was set apart for him, described as "holy to the Lord, the firstfruits of his harvest." That phrase is agricultural language. The firstfruits were the earliest part of the crop, given to God as a sign that the whole harvest belonged to him. Israel was God's firstfruits among the nations, a sign that he intended to bless the whole world through this one people.

And God had protected them fiercely. Anyone who threatened Israel faced disaster. The Egyptians learned that the hard way.

But the honeymoon was over. And what came next broke God's heart.

WHAT WENT WRONG

God's next words land like a hammer: "What fault did your ancestors find in me, that they strayed so far from me?" It's a devastating question. God isn't asking for information. He knows the answer. There was no fault. He had done nothing wrong. He had kept every promise, provided every need, loved them without failing. And they left him anyway.

What did they leave him for? "They followed worthless idols and became worthless themselves." That single sentence contains one of the most important insights in the entire book. People become like what they worship. The Israelites chased after gods that were empty, and they became empty. They devoted themselves to things with no substance, and their own lives lost substance. They bowed down to things they had carved with their own hands, and in doing so, they shrank themselves down to the size of their creations.

God walks through the evidence. He reminds them of everything he had done: rescued them from Egypt, guided them through a wilderness so harsh that no one else would travel through it, brought them into a rich and fertile land. And what did they do with that land? "You came and defiled my land and made my inheritance detestable."

Then God turns his attention to the leaders, the people who should have known better. The priests stopped asking, "Where is the Lord?" The teachers of the law didn't actually know God. The political leaders rebelled against him. And the prophets, the people whose entire job was to speak for God, started prophesying in the name of Baal instead.

From top to bottom, the nation had drifted away from the God who made them.

THE SPRING AND THE CISTERNS

Then comes the image that defines this entire section. God says his people have committed two sins, and he describes them through a picture so vivid you can feel the dust in your throat.

"My people have forsaken me, the spring of living water, and have dug their own cisterns, broken cisterns that cannot hold water."

In the ancient world, a natural spring was the most valuable thing a farmer could have. Fresh water, flowing endlessly from the ground, year after year, no matter how dry the season. You could build your entire life around a spring like that. It would never run out. It would never fail.

A cistern was the opposite. It was a hole carved into rock, sealed with plaster, designed to catch rainwater and store it. Cisterns were common because springs were rare. But the water in a cistern was stale, often contaminated, and the plaster lining could crack, letting all the water drain away into the ground. After all the backbreaking work of carving it out, you could end up with nothing but a dry hole.

Now imagine someone who had a spring, an actual, flowing, never-ending spring of fresh water, and walked away from it. Then imagine that same person spending years hacking a cistern out of solid rock, only to have it crack and leak. That is what Israel did. They abandoned the living God, the source of everything that makes life worth living, and replaced him with gods they had built with their own hands. Gods that couldn't save, couldn't provide, couldn't satisfy. Gods that cracked under pressure and left them with nothing.

Jesus would pick up this exact image centuries later. "If anyone is thirsty," he said, "let him come to me and drink." He was offering himself as the spring Jeremiah described, the living water that never runs dry.

THE UNFAITHFUL BRIDE

What follows is a flood of images, each one more painful than the last. God describes Israel's unfaithfulness from every possible angle.

They were like an ox that threw off its yoke and refused to serve. Like a carefully cultivated vine that reverted to a wild plant producing useless fruit. Like someone scrubbing themselves with the strongest soap available, but the stain of their guilt wouldn't come out. Like a bride who forgot her wedding dress, something no bride in history has ever done. Yet God's people forgot him "days without number."

The most disturbing images compare Israel to someone in the grip of an addiction. God pleads with them to stop chasing after foreign gods, but they respond with the words of someone who has lost control: "It's no use! I love foreign gods, and I must go after them." They know what they're doing is destroying them, and they can't stop.

And then, in a twist that reveals just how confused sin makes people, they turn around and claim they've done nothing wrong. "I am innocent," they say. "He is not angry with me. I have not sinned." The same people who just admitted they couldn't stop chasing idols now deny they were ever chasing them at all. That's what prolonged rebellion does to the human mind. It scrambles your ability to see yourself clearly.

Meanwhile, Israel was also trying to secure its safety by making political alliances with Egypt and Assyria, the great empires to the south and northeast. God saw this for what it was: another form of unfaithfulness. Instead of trusting the God who had rescued them from Egypt, they were running back to Egypt for protection. Instead of relying on the God who had defeated empires on their behalf, they were cutting deals with empires. It was like leaving the spring to drink from a polluted river.

God's verdict was blunt: "Your wickedness will punish you; your backsliding will rebuke you. Consider then and realize how evil and bitter it is for you when you forsake the Lord your God."

CAN THEY COME BACK?

By the beginning of chapter 3, the situation looks hopeless. God raises a legal question drawn from Israel's own law. Under the law of Moses, if a man divorced his wife and she married another man, the first husband could never take her back. That was the rule. It was designed to protect women from being treated like property, tossed back and forth between men.

But here was the problem. Israel hadn't just been unfaithful with one other "husband." She had run after countless lovers. If even one remarriage made reconciliation impossible under the law, what hope was there for a people who had been this unfaithful?

The answer, it turns out, is grace. Grace that goes beyond what the law allows. Grace that takes the initiative even when the offending party has no right to ask for it.

Three times in chapter 3, God says the same thing: "Return." Come back. Come home. He calls Israel "faithless," but in the same breath he invites them to return. He says, "I am faithful. I will not be angry forever. Only acknowledge your guilt." The condition isn't complicated. No elaborate ritual. No impossible task. Just honesty. Admit what you've done. Stop pretending. Face the truth, and the door home swings open.

God even provides a script for what true repentance sounds like: "Surely the idols on the hills and mountains are a lie; surely in the Lord our God is the salvation of Israel. From our youth, shameful gods have consumed the fruits of our fathers' labor. Let us lie down in our shame, and let our disgrace cover us. We have sinned against the Lord our God."

That's real repentance. No excuses. No blame-shifting. No "it wasn't that bad." Just the raw truth spoken out loud. And God promises that if they return to him with genuine repentance, not just outward religious activity but real change in how they live and treat each other, the results would ripple outward to bless the entire world. "Then the nations will be blessed by him."

Israel's repentance wasn't just about Israel. It was about the mission God had given them from the beginning: to be the people through whom he blessed every nation on earth.

THE STORM FROM THE NORTH

But the people didn't return. They didn't repent. And so the final movement of this section—stretching through chapters 4, 5, and 6—shifts from pleading to warning. The tone grows darker. The images grow more terrifying. A storm is gathering in the north, and if the people won't turn back to God, it will sweep them away.

Jeremiah describes an invasion so devastating it looks like creation running in reverse. "I looked at the earth, and it was formless and empty; and at the heavens, and their light was gone. I looked at the mountains, and they were quaking. I looked, and there were no people; every bird in the sky had flown away." The language deliberately echoes Genesis 1, the creation account. What God had built, sin was unbuilding.

God sends Jeremiah on a mission through the streets of Jerusalem: "If you can find but one person who deals honestly and seeks the truth, I will forgive this city." One honest person. That's all God needed. Jeremiah searched among the poor and then among the powerful. Both groups had broken free of God's authority. Both had abandoned the covenant.

The leaders come in for the harshest criticism. The prophets and priests were telling the people exactly what they wanted to hear: "Peace, peace," they said, "when there is no peace." They were treating a fatal wound with a bandage and calling it healed. Worse, the people loved it. "A horrible and shocking thing has happened in the land," God said. "The prophets prophesy lies, the priests rule by their own authority, and my people love it this way."

There's something uniquely dangerous about a culture where everyone, leaders and ordinary people alike, has agreed to believe comfortable lies instead of hard truth. Jeremiah could see it clearly. Nobody else wanted to look.

God offered one final invitation. "Stand at the crossroads and look; ask for the ancient paths, ask where the good way is, and walk in it, and you will find rest for your souls." The ancient paths meant the original covenant faith, the way of life God had given them at Sinai. The path was still there. Rest was still available. All they had to do was walk in it.

Their answer was chilling: "We will not walk in it."

God sent watchmen, prophets to sound the alarm. Their answer was the same: "We will not listen."

The section ends with Jeremiah being compared to a metalworker testing ore in a furnace, trying to refine silver from raw metal. But no matter how hot the fire burned, no matter how hard the bellows blew, the refining produced nothing. The impurities wouldn't separate. The ore was worthless. "They are called rejected silver, because the Lord has rejected them."

It was, for the moment, the end of the conversation.

WHAT THIS MEANS FOR US

First, people become like what they worship. Israel chased after empty gods and became empty themselves. This principle hasn't changed. Whatever you give your deepest attention and devotion to will shape who you become. If you pour your life into things that have no lasting value, don't be surprised when your life starts to feel hollow. What you worship, you become.

Second, God's gifts are not substitutes for God himself. Israel had the land, the temple, the law, the priesthood. They had everything God had given them but had lost the Giver. It's possible to be surrounded by religious activity and Bible knowledge and church involvement and still not know God. The gifts are meant to lead you to the one who gave them.

Third, real repentance is honest, specific, and life-changing. God didn't ask for better rituals or more elaborate sacrifices. He asked for honesty: "Acknowledge your guilt." True repentance doesn't make excuses or minimize what went wrong. It faces the truth and then turns in a new direction. And real repentance shows up in how you treat people, not just in how you worship.

Fourth, comfortable lies are more dangerous than hard truths. The false prophets told the people what they wanted to hear: everything is fine, God isn't angry, peace is coming. The people loved it. But it was killing them. When someone tells you only what you want to hear, be careful. A real friend, and a real God, will tell you what you need to hear, even when it hurts.

Fifth, there is always a way back. Even after everything Israel had done, God said, "Return." Three times. The door was open. The spring was still flowing. No matter how far you've wandered, the invitation still stands. Come home.

TALKING POINTS

1. **God described Israel's sin as leaving a spring of living water to dig broken cisterns.** What are some "broken cisterns" people chase after today, things that promise satisfaction but can never deliver? Why do you think people keep going back to them even after being disappointed?

2. **God said his people "became worthless" because they followed worthless idols.** What does it mean that people become like what they worship? Can you think of examples where someone's priorities shaped who they became, for better or worse?

3. **The people of Judah swung back and forth between admitting they couldn't stop sinning and claiming they hadn't sinned at all.** Why is it so hard to be honest about our failures? What makes denial so tempting?

4. **The prophets and priests told the people "Peace, peace" when there was no peace.** Why is it dangerous when leaders only tell people what they want to hear? How can you tell the difference between someone who is encouraging you and someone who is just avoiding the truth?

5. **God told the people to "stand at the crossroads and look; ask for the ancient paths." They refused.** What "ancient paths" do you think God might be calling his people back to today? What makes it hard to follow a path that everyone else has abandoned?

The people had heard the warning. They had been shown the ancient paths. They had been offered living water, an open door, a way home. And they said no. The prophets kept preaching peace. The priests kept going through the motions. The people kept chasing after gods made of wood and stone.

But Jeremiah wasn't done. God had more to say, and the temple itself was about to become the stage for the most dangerous sermon of the prophet's life.

Turn the page.

3

THE SERMON THAT ALMOST GOT HIM KILLED

Have you ever known someone who thought a lucky charm could protect them? Maybe they had a pair of lucky socks they wore to every game, or a bracelet they refused to take off before a test. As long as they had the charm, they felt safe. It didn't matter if they hadn't studied or practiced. The charm was their security blanket.

Now imagine an entire nation doing the same thing, except instead of lucky socks, it was a building. The most important building in their world. The temple of God.

The people of Judah believed that as long as the temple stood in Jerusalem, God would never let anything bad happen to them. It didn't matter how they lived. It didn't matter if they cheated the poor, worshiped other gods, or broke every commandment God had ever given them. The temple was their lucky charm. God lived there. He would protect his own house, and everyone in it, no matter what.

Jeremiah was about to walk into the busiest entrance of that building and tell them they were dead wrong. And he would almost die for it.

STANDING AT THE GATE

God's instructions were specific. Go to the gate of the temple and preach. Not in a back room. Not to a small group. Stand where the crowds pour in and deliver this message where everyone can hear it. The gate would have been packed with worshipers arriving for a festival, streaming through the entrance with their sacrifices and offerings, confident that their religious routines were keeping them in God's good graces.

Jeremiah planted himself in the middle of all that traffic and opened his mouth.

His sermon had two main points, and both of them were explosive. First, a command: change your ways and your actions, and God will let you go on living in this place. Second, a warning: stop trusting in deceptive words. Specifically, stop chanting, "This is the temple of the Lord, the temple of the Lord, the temple of the Lord."

The people had turned that phrase into a kind of magic spell. They repeated it three times, as if saying it enough would make it work. This is God's temple. God won't let anything happen to it. We're safe.

Jeremiah called it a lie.

Not because the building wasn't the temple. It was. Solomon had built it centuries earlier. God's presence really did dwell there. But the people had twisted a truth into a deception. They had taken a real fact about God's house and turned it into an insurance policy that covered them no matter how they behaved. They thought the building itself guaranteed their safety, regardless of whether they actually obeyed the God who lived in it.

Jeremiah laid out what God actually required, and none of it had anything to do with showing up at the temple on the right day with the right sacrifice. God wanted them to deal with each other justly. Stop oppressing foreigners, orphans, and widows. Stop shedding innocent blood. Stop running after other gods. These were the covenant conditions for living in God's land. They had been spelled out since the days of Moses. And the people were ignoring every one of them.

Then, six days a week, they would steal, murder, commit adultery, lie under oath, and burn incense to other gods. And on the seventh day they would walk into the temple and say, "We are safe." Jeremiah's response was scorching: "Has this house, which bears my Name, become a den of robbers to you?"

Think about what that phrase means. A den of robbers isn't where robbers do their stealing. It's where they go to hide after they've stolen. Jeremiah was saying that the people were using God's temple the same way criminals use a hideout. They would commit their crimes all week and then flee to the temple for cover, as if God couldn't see what they had been doing Sunday through Friday just because they showed up on the Sabbath.

Jesus would quote this exact verse centuries later when he overturned the tables in the temple courts. The same sickness Jeremiah diagnosed was still alive in Jesus' day: religious activity divorced from actual obedience, sacred buildings used as shields against the consequences of ungodly living.

REMEMBER SHILOH

Then Jeremiah dropped a bomb. "Go now to the place in Shiloh where I first made a dwelling for my Name, and see what I did to it because of the wickedness of my people Israel."

Shiloh. The name would have hit the crowd like a punch. Shiloh had been God's home before Jerusalem. Centuries earlier, the tabernacle had been stationed there. The ark of the covenant had rested there. It was the spiritual center of the nation during the time of Samuel.

And it was gone. Destroyed, probably by the Philistines. By Jeremiah's day, Shiloh was nothing but overgrown ruins, a few crumbling walls in a field. A place where God had once lived, abandoned to weeds and silence.

The people of Jerusalem knew what had happened to Shiloh, but they thought it proved they were special. Shiloh was in the north. The northern kingdom had been wicked, and God had destroyed them. But Jerusalem was different. Jerusalem had the temple. Jerusalem had God's promise to David. Jerusalem was untouchable.

Jeremiah said, "Look at Shiloh. That's your future."

The crowd nearly killed him for it. Chapter 26 tells us what happened next: the priests and prophets and people seized him and said, "You must die! How dare you say this house will be like Shiloh?" It took the intervention of some government officials and the memory of an earlier prophet who had said something similar to save Jeremiah's life. He walked away from the temple that day knowing that the people had heard God's message and chosen to reject it.

But for those who would later read this sermon in exile,

sitting in Babylon surrounded by the rubble of everything Jeremiah had warned about, the message would have carried a strange kind of hope. If God wasn't bound to Shiloh, and he wasn't bound to the Jerusalem temple, then his presence wasn't tied to any building at all. God could meet his people anywhere. Even in Babylon.

A PEOPLE WHO WON'T LISTEN

The rest of chapter 7 widens the accusation. God tells Jeremiah to stop praying for these people. That's a startling command. Prophets were supposed to pray. Moses had done it. Samuel had done it. But these people were so far gone in their rebellion that God said, in effect, "Don't waste your prayers. I won't answer them."

Then God described what was happening behind the closed doors of ordinary Israelite homes. Whole families were participating in the worship of foreign gods. Children gathered wood. Fathers lit fires. Mothers kneaded dough to bake cakes shaped like the "Queen of Heaven," a foreign goddess. The idolatry had become normal family life. Children grew up thinking this was just how things worked. Nobody questioned it.

And the worst part was still to come. God said, "They have built the high places of Topheth in the Valley of Ben Hinnom to burn their sons and daughters in the fire, something I did not command, nor did it enter my mind." Child sacrifice. The people of God had sunk to the same practices that had caused God to drive out the Canaanites before them. They were killing their own children for gods made of wood and stone.

The chapter closes with a devastating summary. God had been sending his prophets to this people since the day he brought them out of Egypt. "Again and again I sent my servants the prophets," God said. "But they did not listen to me or pay attention. They were stiff-necked and did more evil than their ancestors."

Generation after generation. Century after century. The same message, delivered by prophet after prophet. And the same response: deaf ears and hard hearts.

TEARS WITHOUT END

Chapters 8–9 plunge us back into the emotional depths of the book. These are some of the passages that earned Jeremiah the title "the weeping prophet."

The poetry is relentless. God points out that even migrating birds know when to fly south for winter and when to come back. They follow their instincts perfectly, every single year. But God's own people "do not know the requirements of the Lord." Animals are more reliable than the nation of Israel.

The leaders come under fire again. The teachers of the law claimed to possess God's word, but they had twisted it into something harmless, using clever interpretations to avoid the hard demands of the covenant. "Peace, peace," they kept telling the people, "when there is no peace." They were doctors who looked at a gaping, infected wound and said, "It's just a scratch." The people believed them because the lie was so much more comfortable than the truth.

Then comes a passage so raw it takes your breath away. The voice shifts between Jeremiah and God so seamlessly that scholars still debate who is speaking in certain lines. And maybe that's the point. The pain of the prophet and the pain of God had become indistinguishable.

"Since my people are crushed, I am crushed; I mourn, and horror grips me. Is there no balm in Gilead? Is there no physician there? Why then is there no healing for the wound of my people?"

Gilead was a region known for producing medicinal balm, a healing ointment. Jeremiah's question isn't about a lack of medicine. It's about a wound so deep that no remedy can reach it. The sickness of this nation has gone past the point where any treatment can help.

And then: "Oh, that my head were a spring of water and my eyes a fountain of tears! I would weep day and night for the slain of my people."

There aren't enough tears. The grief is bottomless. The prophet needs an ocean's worth of weeping and doesn't have it. He needs more tears than a human body can produce. Because what is coming will be so terrible, so devastating, that no amount of mourning will be adequate to the scale of the loss.

God's grief is woven through these same verses. He looks at the wreckage of his people's culture, where lying has become an art form and no one can trust a neighbor or even a family member, and he says, "Should I not punish them for this? Should I not avenge myself on such a nation as this?" The questions aren't eager. They're exhausted. God is asking, "What else can I possibly do? What other option have you left me?"

Then, in the middle of all this grief, two verses shine out like a lantern in a dark room. God says: "Let not the wise boast of their wisdom or the strong boast of their strength or the rich boast of their riches, but let the one who boasts boast about this: that they have the understanding to know me, that I am the Lord, who exercises kindness, justice and righteousness on earth, for in these I delight."

That's the whole point. Stripped of every false security, every lucky charm, every lie about peace and safety, here is what remains: knowing God. Not just knowing *about* him. Knowing him, his character, his kindness, his justice, his righteousness. Everything else will fail. Wisdom, strength, and riches will all crumble. But knowing the living God is the one thing that endures.

THE SCARECROW AND THE GOD OF THUNDER

Chapter 10 delivers the final contrast. Jeremiah sets the living God side by side with the idols the nations worship, and the comparison is devastating.

He describes how the nations cut down a tree, hand it to a craftsman, cover it with silver and gold, and nail it to a stand so it won't topple over. Then they bow down before it.

Jeremiah's verdict: "Like a scarecrow in a cucumber field, their idols cannot speak; they must be carried because they cannot walk. Do not fear them; they can do no harm nor can they do any good."

A scarecrow. That's what the gods of the nations amount to. Something propped up in a field to frighten birds. It can't speak. It can't move. It can't help. It can't hurt. It can't "while away the hours, conferrin' with the flowers, consultin' with the rain." It's just fabric and sticks dressed up to look impressive. You might be fooled from a distance, but up close, there's nothing there.

Against this pathetic picture, Jeremiah sets the God of Israel, and the contrast is like placing a candle next to the sun. The true God made the heavens and the earth. He established the world by his wisdom. When he thunders, the waters in the sky roar. He makes clouds rise from the ends of the earth. He sends lightning with the rain and brings out the wind from his storehouses.

Every idol-maker, Jeremiah says, is shamed by his images. They are a fraud. There is no breath in them. They are worthless, objects of mockery. When their day of reckoning comes, they will perish.

"But he who is the Portion of Jacob is not like these, for he is the Maker of all things."

The chapter, and this whole section of the book, closes with a prayer. Jeremiah knows what is coming. He knows the armies from the north are on their way. He knows the people won't repent. So he prays for mercy in the middle of judgment: "Correct me, Lord, but only in due measure, not in your anger, or you will reduce me to nothing."

Even now, even at the darkest point, the prophet is holding onto the one thing that cannot be taken away: the character of a God who is just and merciful at the same time.

WHAT THIS MEANS FOR US

First, religious activity is no substitute for obedience. The people of Judah thought showing up at the temple would protect them, even while they ignored everything God asked of them. Going to church, reading your Bible, worshiping the right way on Sunday means nothing if the rest of your week contradicts all of it. God has never been impressed by rituals performed by people who refuse to live differently.

Second, no building, institution, or tradition is too sacred for God to remove. The temple was the most important building in Israel's history, and God let it be destroyed. If you think any church, organization, or movement is untouchable just because God used it in the past, remember Shiloh. God is not bound to any structure. He is bound to his character and his promises.

Third, comfortable lies are deadlier than painful truths. The prophets who said "Peace, peace" were more popular than Jeremiah. They told the people what they wanted to hear. But their comfortable words led to destruction, while Jeremiah's painful words could have led to life, if anyone had listened. Be suspicious of anyone who only ever tells you good news.

Fourth, knowing God matters more than anything else you could boast about. Not your intelligence. Not your strength. Not your money. Knowing the God who exercises kindness, justice, and righteousness. That's the one boast that survives when everything else falls apart.

Fifth, God's judgment is real, but so is his grief. These chapters don't show us a God who punishes coldly and moves on. They show us a God weeping over the very people he is forced to judge. His anger and his tears flow from the same source: a love so deep that betrayal produces both fury and heartbreak at once.

TALKING POINTS

1. **The people chanted "The temple of the Lord" as if the building itself would save them.** What are some things people trust in today for security that aren't the same as actually trusting God? How can good things become substitutes for a real relationship with him?

2. **Jeremiah compared the temple to "a den of robbers,"**

a hideout for criminals. What would it look like for someone to use church or religious activities as a "hideout" today, going through the motions to feel safe while ignoring how they actually live?

3. **God asked, "Is there no balm in Gilead?" about the wounds of his people.** What do you think it means when a problem has gone so deep that normal remedies can't fix it? Have you ever seen a situation where the real problem was being ignored while people treated the symptoms?

4. **Jeremiah described the idols of the nations as scarecrows in a field. They look impressive but can't do anything.** What are some modern "scarecrows" that people treat as powerful or important but that are actually powerless to help when it really matters?

5. **God said, "Let the one who boasts boast about this: that they have the understanding to know me."** Why is knowing God described as the one thing worth boasting about? What's the difference between knowing about God and actually knowing him?

The temple sermon had been preached. The idols had been exposed as scarecrows. The tears had been shed. And still the people refused to listen. God had warned them through the law, through the prophets, through the ruins of Shiloh, through Jeremiah himself. Now the prophet's message was about to become even more personal, as God told him to stop building a normal life altogether and as the pain of speaking for God began to tear Jeremiah apart from the inside.

Turn the page.

4

THE COST OF SPEAKING UP

Picture this. You're at school and you see something wrong. Maybe someone is cheating. Maybe a group of kids is ganging up on someone who can't fight back. Maybe a rumor is spreading that you know isn't true. You have a choice: say something or stay quiet.

You decide to speak up. And at first, it goes about as badly as you'd expect. The people doing wrong get angry. They push back. They call you names.

But then something worse happens. The people you thought were on your side turn against you too. Your friends go quiet. The kid you defended doesn't back you up. Someone in your own family tells you to stop making trouble, that you're embarrassing them. The very people who should have stood with you are now the ones making your life miserable.

That kind of betrayal cuts deeper than anything an enemy can do. An enemy's hostility makes sense. But when the people closest to you turn on you for doing the right thing, it makes you wonder if doing the right thing is even worth it.

Jeremiah found out.

Chapters 11–20 of Jeremiah are the most personal sections of the entire book. Up to this point, we've mostly heard Jeremiah delivering God's messages to the nation. But now the camera turns inward. We see what it cost this man to be God's prophet. We hear his private conversations with God, conversations so raw and honest they would shock most people. We watch him lose his family, his community, his safety, and nearly his sanity. We see him beaten, locked in stocks, and plotted against by the most powerful people in the nation.

And through it all, we hear two voices crying out in pain: the voice of the prophet and the voice of God. Sometimes it's impossible to tell them apart.

THE COVENANT IS BROKEN

Chapter 11 opens with a sermon that would have been familiar in tone to anyone who had heard Jeremiah preach before. God tells him to remind the people of the covenant, the agreement God made with Israel at Mount Sinai after the exodus from Egypt. The terms were simple. God had rescued them. He had given them a land flowing with milk and honey. In return, they were to obey his commands and have no other gods.

But the people had broken that covenant, systematically and deliberately, for generations. The word "listen" echoes through this passage like a drumbeat. God told them to listen. They did not listen. He sent prophets. They did not listen. He warned them again and again. They still did not listen.

And now, for the first time, Jeremiah states it in the plainest possible terms: "Both Israel and Judah have broken the covenant I made with their ancestors." The covenant wasn't just fraying at the edges. It was shattered. And with it shattered, all that remained were the consequences that the covenant itself had promised for those who broke it.

God told Jeremiah, again, to stop praying for these people. That command tells you something about Jeremiah. He was still praying for them. Even after years of rejection, even after being mocked and threatened, he was still on his knees asking God to spare the very people who hated him.

BETRAYED BY FAMILY

Then came the blow Jeremiah never saw coming. God revealed to him that there was a plot against his life, and it wasn't coming from the government or the religious establishment. It was coming from his own village. His own family. The people of Anathoth, the town where he had grown up, wanted him dead.

"Let us destroy the tree and its fruit," they said. "Let us cut him off from the land of the living, that his name be remembered no more."

Jeremiah said he had been like "a gentle lamb led to the slaughter." He hadn't even suspected the plot until God warned him about it. The people he had grown up with, the people who shared his bloodline, were conspiring to kill him because his preaching threatened everything they held dear.

Why would his own family turn on him? Probably because Jeremiah's message attacked the very foundations of their world. He had said the temple was a lie. He had said the covenant was broken. He had said the land would be taken away. For a priestly family in a small village, whose entire identity and livelihood were wrapped up in those things, Jeremiah's preaching must have felt like a direct assault on their survival. They didn't see a prophet speaking God's truth. They saw a traitor tearing apart everything they believed in.

Jeremiah's response was to take his case to God. He didn't retaliate. He didn't plot his own revenge. He went to the divine Judge and asked for justice.

But he also asked a question that has haunted believers for thousands of years.

WHY DO THE WICKED PROSPER?

"You are always righteous, Lord, when I bring a case before you. Yet I would speak with you about your justice: Why does the way of the wicked prosper? Why do all the faithless live at ease?"

Jeremiah trusted that God was just. He believed it in his bones. But the evidence in front of his eyes didn't match what he believed. The people who were trying to kill him were doing fine. The leaders who lied to the nation were living comfortably. The prophets who told people what they wanted to hear were popular and well-fed. Meanwhile, Jeremiah, the one person in the country telling the truth, was broke, alone, hated, and in danger of being murdered by his own relatives.

It's one of the oldest questions in the world. Why do bad people seem to get away with it? Why does doing the right thing sometimes make your life worse instead of better?

God's answer to Jeremiah was not what he was hoping for. God didn't explain the mystery of injustice. He didn't promise that things would get easier. He essentially said, "If you think this is hard, it's about to get harder. If you can't handle running with men on foot, how will you keep up when you're racing against horses?"

Not exactly comforting. But there's something important buried in that response. God didn't deny Jeremiah's pain. He didn't dismiss the question. He simply told the truth: the road ahead would be even more difficult, and Jeremiah needed to be ready.

A LIFE SET APART

Then God demanded something that would have seemed almost cruel. He told Jeremiah not to get married. Not to have children. Not to attend funerals in the community. Not to go to wedding celebrations. Not to participate in any of the normal social activities that made a person part of their community.

For a young man in ancient Israel, this was devastating. Marriage and children weren't optional extras. They were the foundation of normal life. A man without a wife and children was an oddity, a source of gossip and suspicion. And to refuse to show up at funerals and weddings was socially unforgivable. Those were the moments when communities came together. To be absent was to insult every family in the village.

But that was exactly the point. Jeremiah's enforced isolation was itself a message. His empty house was a preview of the empty houses that would fill the land when the invasion came. His absence from funerals was a picture of a day when death would be so widespread that no one would be left to mourn. His absence from weddings was a forecast of a time when there would be no more joy, no more celebration, no more laughter in the streets of Judah.

Jeremiah didn't just speak God's message. He lived it. His whole existence became a walking sermon, and the cost was a loneliness so deep it nearly destroyed him.

THE POTTER AND THE CLAY

In the middle of all this personal anguish, God sent Jeremiah on an errand that would produce one of the most famous images in the Bible. "Go down to the potter's house," God said, "and there I will give you my message."

Jeremiah went and watched the potter at work. The craftsman was shaping a lump of clay on his wheel, working it into a vessel. But something went wrong. Maybe there was a flaw in the clay, maybe it wasn't cooperating with the potter's design. Whatever the reason, the potter didn't throw the clay away. He pressed it back down and started over, reshaping it into a different vessel, whatever seemed best to him.

God's message was this: "Can I not do with you, Israel, as this potter does? Like clay in the hand of the potter, so are you in my hand."

But here's what makes this passage so surprising. God wasn't just saying, "I'm in charge and you can't stop me." He was saying something much more nuanced. He was saying that he responds to what people do. If he announces judgment against a nation and that nation repents, he will relent and not carry out the judgment. If he promises blessing to a nation and that nation turns to evil, he will reconsider the blessing.

God was offering Judah one more chance. "I am preparing a disaster for you," he said. "So turn from your evil ways, each one of you, and reform your ways and your actions."

The people's response was the most chilling sentence in the book so far: "It's no use. We will continue with our own plans; each of us will follow the stubbornness of our evil hearts."

They knew what they were doing. They admitted it. And they chose to keep doing it anyway.

THE SMASHED JAR

After the potter's wheel came the potter's shop. God told Jeremiah to buy a large clay jar, gather some elders and priests, and take them to the Valley of Ben Hinnom, the city's garbage dump outside the walls. There, standing among the broken pottery and rotting refuse, Jeremiah delivered a message of final judgment.

Then he raised the jar over his head and smashed it on the ground. "This is what the Lord Almighty says: I will smash this nation and this city just as this potter's jar is smashed and cannot be repaired."

The difference between the two pottery illustrations was deliberate and devastating. At the potter's wheel, the clay was still soft. It could be reshaped. There was still time to change. But a fired pot that has been smashed on the ground cannot be put back together. The pieces are beyond repair. The time for reshaping was over. The people had made their choice, and the consequences were now locked in.

Jeremiah then walked back into the temple courtyard and repeated the message to everyone there. It was the bravest and most dangerous thing he had done since the temple sermon years earlier.

BEATEN BUT NOT SILENCED

The response was immediate. Pashhur, the chief officer of the temple, had Jeremiah beaten and locked in stocks overnight. It was the first time Jeremiah suffered official, physical punishment for his preaching. It would not be the last.

When Pashhur released him the next morning, Jeremiah didn't apologize. He didn't tone down his message. He looked Pashhur in the eye and told him that God had renamed him "Terror on Every Side," because Pashhur himself would live to see the terror of Babylon's invasion. And for the first time in the book, Jeremiah named the enemy out loud: Babylon. The unnamed threat from the north finally had a name.

THE BREAKING POINT

What follows is the rawest passage in the entire book, and one of the most startlingly honest prayers in all of Scripture. Jeremiah 20:7–18 is the last of Jeremiah's personal laments, and it reads like the words of a man who has been pushed to the very edge of what a human being can endure.

"You deceived me, Lord, and I was deceived; you overpowered me and prevailed."

The word translated "deceived" is shockingly strong. Jeremiah felt tricked, lured into a calling that had consumed his entire life and left him with nothing but pain. Every day people ridiculed him. Every time he opened his mouth to deliver God's message, it brought him more hatred and rejection. He tried to stop. He told himself he would never speak in God's name again. But the message burned inside him like a fire in his bones, and he couldn't hold it in.

"I am ridiculed all day long; everyone mocks me," he said. "The word of the Lord has brought me insult and reproach all day long. But if I say, 'I will not mention his word or speak anymore in his name,' his word is in my heart like a fire, a fire shut up in my bones. I am weary of holding it in; indeed, I cannot."

He was trapped. Speaking up brought suffering from people. Staying silent brought agony from within. There was no escape, no comfortable option, no way out.

And then, in one of the most astonishing turns in the Bible, Jeremiah swings from despair to faith in a single breath. "But the Lord is with me like a mighty warrior; so my persecutors will stumble and not prevail." In the very same prayer where he accuses God of tricking him, he declares that God is his defender. The man who feels abandoned by God still believes God will save him.

And then he swings again, this time into the darkest words any prophet ever spoke. "Cursed be the day I was born! May the day my mother bore me not be blessed! Why did I ever come out of the womb to see trouble and sorrow and to end my days in shame?"

Jeremiah didn't want to die. He wished he had never been born. He wished the whole story of his life had never started, because the calling that defined his existence had become unbearable.

These words are in the Bible. God allowed them to be preserved, not because they represent the right way to think about God, but because they represent the honest truth of what one faithful man felt in the darkest moment of his life. And if the Bible has room for that kind of honesty, then there is room in your relationship with God for honesty too.

WHAT THIS MEANS FOR US

First, speaking the truth can cost you everything. Jeremiah lost his family, his community, his social life, his safety, and very nearly his sanity because he refused to stop telling the truth. Nobody promised that faithfulness would be comfortable. Sometimes doing the right thing makes your life harder, not easier.

Second, it's okay to be honest with God about your pain. Jeremiah accused God of tricking him. He wished he'd never been born. He questioned God's justice. And God didn't strike him down for it. God can handle your honesty. What he can't work with is your pretending.

Third, the wicked don't prosper forever. Jeremiah asked why the faithless live at ease, and it's a question every generation asks. The Bible's answer isn't that justice always comes quickly. Sometimes it takes longer than we can stand. But it does come. God sees, and God acts, even when the timeline doesn't match ours.

Fourth, there comes a point when soft clay becomes a smashed pot. The potter's wheel and the smashed jar tell the same story from two different moments. While there's still time, change is possible. But stubbornness has consequences that eventually become irreversible. Don't wait until the clay has hardened.

Fifth, faith and doubt can exist in the same person at the same time. Jeremiah accused God and praised God in the same prayer. He felt abandoned and protected in the same breath. If your faith feels messy and contradictory, you're in the company of one of the greatest prophets who ever lived. God doesn't need your faith to be tidy. He just needs it to be real.

TALKING POINTS

1. **Jeremiah was betrayed by his own family because his message threatened their way of life.** Have you ever experienced pushback from people close to you for saying something true? What makes it harder when the opposition comes from people you love?

2. **Jeremiah asked God, "Why does the way of the wicked prosper?" and God's answer was essentially, "It's going to get harder."** Why do you think God didn't give Jeremiah a more comforting answer? What does that tell us about what God values more: our comfort, or our faithfulness?

3. **God told Jeremiah not to marry, attend funerals, or go to parties. His whole life became a living message.** What would it look like for your life to be a message to the people around you? What are the costs of living that way?

4. **The potter's wheel showed that God is willing to reshape his plans based on how people respond. The smashed jar showed that there comes a point when reshaping is no longer possible.** How do you know when you're still on the wheel and when you're getting close to the point of no return?

5. **Jeremiah said God's word was "like a fire shut up in my bones." He couldn't stop speaking even though it brought him nothing but pain.** Have you ever felt compelled to do something you knew was right, even though it cost you? What kept you going?

Jeremiah had been beaten, betrayed, isolated, and pushed to the breaking point. His own people had rejected every word God spoke through him. The nation was hurtling toward destruction, and now even the prophet himself was crying out in anguish.

But God wasn't finished speaking. Jeremiah still had messages to deliver, and some of them would be aimed directly at the kings and prophets who had led the nation to ruin.

Turn the page.

5

KINGS AND FALSE PROPHETS

You probably know the story of "The Emperor's New Clothes" by Hans Christian Andersen. Two con artists show up in a kingdom claiming they can weave the most magnificent fabric in the world. They tell the emperor that only wise and competent people can see it. Fools and incompetent people see nothing at all.

So when the emperor and his advisors go to inspect the loom and find it completely empty, nobody says a word. Nobody wants to be the fool. Everyone nods and smiles and compliments the invisible fabric. The emperor parades through the streets wearing nothing at all, and the entire kingdom plays along, because telling the truth would mean admitting what nobody wants to admit.

Until a child in the crowd says what everyone can see: "But he hasn't got anything on!"

That child is Jeremiah.

Chapters 21–29 place Jeremiah in direct conflict with the two most powerful groups in the nation: the kings who ruled and the prophets who told those kings exactly what they wanted to hear. Everyone around Jeremiah was playing along with the lie that things were fine, that God would protect Jerusalem no matter what, that the crisis would pass quickly and everything would go back to normal.

Jeremiah was the only one saying the emperor had no clothes. And it nearly got him killed. Again.

A PARADE OF BAD KINGS

These chapters contain Jeremiah's report card on the kings of Judah, and the grades are devastating. The section is organized not by when the kings ruled, but by the message God wanted to make through each of their stories.

It opens with the last king, Zedekiah, because his situation was the most desperate. Babylon's armies were closing in on Jerusalem, and Zedekiah sent messengers to Jeremiah with a request that dripped with irony: "Please ask God for a miracle. Maybe the Lord will do wonders for us, like in the old days."

Think about that. For decades, the government had ignored, mocked, and imprisoned the prophet. Now, with the enemy at the gates, they wanted Jeremiah to put in a good word with the God they had spent their entire reign rejecting. It was like a student who skipped every class all semester asking the teacher for extra credit on the last day.

Jeremiah's answer was the worst news a king could receive. God wasn't going to fight for Jerusalem. God was going to fight against it. "I myself will fight against you with an outstretched hand and mighty arm, in furious anger and in great wrath." The weapons Zedekiah had stockpiled to fight Babylon would be useless, because Babylon wasn't his real problem. God was.

Then Jeremiah stepped back in time to evaluate the kings

who had led the nation to this point. He moved through them like a prosecutor laying out evidence.

Jehoahaz had lasted only three months before Egypt hauled him away into exile. He would never come home.

Jehoiakim was the worst of the bunch, and Jeremiah saved his sharpest words for him. This king had built himself a lavish palace using forced labor, refusing to pay the workers who built it. He decorated his rooms with expensive cedar and painted them bright red, as if he could prove he was a great king by the size of his house. Meanwhile, the poor were being crushed, innocent blood was being shed, and the king's eyes were fixed on nothing but "dishonest gain."

Then Jeremiah pulled out a comparison so sharp it must have cut the air. He pointed to Jehoiakim's own father, King Josiah. "He did what was right and just, so all went well with him. He defended the cause of the poor and needy, and so all went well."

And then came the line that echoes across the centuries: "Is not this what it means to know me?" declares the Lord.

Read that again. God was defining what it means to know him. Not by how much theology you can recite. Not by how many prayers you offer. Not by how impressive your religious credentials are. To know God is to do justice, to care for the poor, to defend the powerless. Josiah knew God because Josiah lived like God. Jehoiakim didn't know God because Jehoiakim lived only for himself.

The final king in the parade was Jehoiachin, Jehoiakim's son, who lasted a mere three months before Nebuchadnezzar carted him off to Babylon. God declared that none of

Jehoiachin's sons would ever sit on the throne of David. The royal line, for all practical purposes, was over.

Or was it?

THE RIGHTEOUS BRANCH

Just when it seemed like there was no future for the line of David, God made a promise that reached far beyond anything Jeremiah's audience could have imagined. After condemning the "shepherds" (kings) who had scattered and destroyed the flock, God said he would raise up a new kind of king. "The days are coming," God declared, "when I will raise up for David a righteous Branch, a King who will reign wisely and do what is just and right in the land. In his days Judah will be saved and Israel will live in safety. This is the name by which he will be called: The Lord Our Righteous Savior."

This was a prophecy of the Messiah. And notice what kind of king God promised. Not a king who would build the biggest palace. Not a king who would crush every enemy with military force. A king who would reign wisely and do what is just and right. A king who would look like Josiah, not Jehoiakim. A king who would actually know God and reflect God's character to the world.

Christians see this promise fulfilled in Jesus, a descendant of David, who reigned not from a throne of gold but from a cross of wood, and whose kingdom would never end.

THE PROPHETS WHO LIED

From kings, Jeremiah turned to the other group responsible for the nation's ruin: the prophets. Chapter 23 contains the most sustained attack on false religious leaders in the entire Old Testament.

These weren't fringe figures. They were the official religious voices of the nation, the people who stood in the temple and said, "This is what the Lord says." They claimed the same authority as Jeremiah. They used the same language. And the ordinary people had no easy way to tell who was telling the truth.

Jeremiah laid out three charges against them.

First, they had no moral integrity. They were guilty of adultery, dishonesty, and corruption. They lived in private sin while making public pronouncements about God. Whatever authority they claimed in the temple evaporated in the way they lived outside it.

Second, they had no moral courage. Instead of challenging the wicked and calling people to repentance, they "strengthened the hands of evildoers, so that not one of them turns from their wickedness." They were spiritual cheerleaders for the status quo. They told people what they wanted to hear, not what they needed to hear. "Peace, peace," they kept saying, when there was no peace.

Third, they had no mandate from God. "I did not send these prophets," God said, "yet they have run with their message. I did not speak to them, yet they have prophesied." They claimed to have dreams and visions from God, but it was all fabricated. God compared the difference between their words and his own to the difference between straw and grain. False teaching might look like something, but there's no nourishment in it. God's word, by contrast, "is like fire, and like a hammer that breaks a rock in pieces."

GOOD FIGS AND BAD FIGS

After Nebuchadnezzar's attack on Jerusalem in 597 BC, in which he carried King Jehoiachin and 10,000 of the nation's leaders into exile, God gave Jeremiah a vision. Two baskets of figs sat in front of the temple. One basket held beautiful, ripe figs. The other held figs so rotten they were inedible.

The popular assumption was obvious. The people left behind in Jerusalem were the good figs. They had been spared. The people taken to Babylon were the bad figs. They had been judged and thrown away.

God flipped the script completely. The good figs were the exiles. The bad figs were the ones left behind. It was one of the most shocking reversals in the entire book. God declared that he would watch over the exiles, bring them back, give them a heart to know him, and restore them. But those left behind would face the full weight of destruction when Babylon came back to finish what it started.

This was an act of pure grace. The exiles hadn't earned their status as "good figs." They were just as guilty as everyone else. But God, for reasons that had nothing to do with their merit, chose to build the future through them.

NEBUCHADNEZZAR AND SEVENTY YEARS

Chapter 25 marks the halfway point of the book and delivers two of Jeremiah's most startling statements.

The first: God called Nebuchadnezzar "my servant." The pagan king of the most powerful empire on earth, the man who would destroy God's temple and carry God's people into captivity, was described as a servant of the Lord. Not because

Nebuchadnezzar worshiped God. He didn't. But because God was using him to accomplish a purpose that no one in Judah wanted to accept. God was sovereign over Nebuchadnezzar whether Nebuchadnezzar knew it or not.

The second: the exile would last seventy years. That was a long time, long enough for two or three generations to be born and die in a foreign land. But it was also a limited time. Babylon's power had an expiration date. And when that date arrived, God would hold Babylon accountable for its own sins. The tool God used for judgment would itself be judged.

THE YOKE AND THE SHOWDOWN

Perhaps the most dramatic scene in this section comes in chapters 27–28. An international conference was being held in Jerusalem, with ambassadors from neighboring nations discussing whether to rebel against Babylon. Jeremiah crashed the meeting wearing an actual ox yoke around his neck, the kind of wooden harness used to hitch oxen to a plow. His message was blunt: submit to Babylon. This is what God requires right now. Anyone who resists will be destroyed.

Then a prophet named Hananiah stepped forward. In front of the priests and all the people, Hananiah made his own prediction: within two years, God would break the yoke of Babylon. The exiles would come home. The king would return. Everything would go back to normal. Then Hananiah grabbed the wooden yoke off Jeremiah's neck and snapped it in two.

Jeremiah's first response was surprising. "Amen! May the Lord do so!" He genuinely wished Hananiah's prediction were true. But then he added a warning: throughout Israel's history, the prophets who came before had mostly prophesied war, disaster, and plague. A prophet who predicts peace carries the burden of proof. Only if it comes true can you know God sent him.

Jeremiah walked away. He didn't argue. He didn't make a scene. He left and waited for God to speak.

God's response came a few days later: the wooden yoke would be replaced by an iron one. Babylon's grip was unbreakable. And Hananiah, the prophet who led the people to trust in lies, was dead within two months.

THE LETTER THAT CHANGED EVERYTHING

Chapter 29 contains what may be the most important letter ever written to a group of refugees. Jeremiah sent it from Jerusalem to the exiles in Babylon, and its message was as shocking as anything he had ever said.

First, settle down. Build houses. Plant gardens. Get married. Have children. Have grandchildren. Don't live as if you're leaving next week. You're going to be there for a long time.

Second, and this was the part that must have made people furious: "Seek the peace and prosperity of the city to which I have carried you into exile. Pray to the Lord for it, because if it prospers, you too will prosper."

Pray for Babylon? Seek the welfare of the enemy? The people who destroyed your homes and dragged you a thousand miles from everything you loved? Jeremiah was asking the exiles to do something that sounded impossible: to love their enemies and pray for those who had conquered them. Centuries later, Jesus would give the same command.

And then came the verse that has been printed on more greeting cards, bookmarks, and coffee mugs than almost any other verse in the Bible: "For I know the plans I have for you," declares the Lord, "plans to prosper you and not to harm you, plans to give you hope and a future."

That verse is beautiful. It's also deeply misunderstood when it's pulled out of context. This wasn't a promise whispered to high school and college graduates to make them feel good. It was a lifeline thrown to people drowning in the worst catastrophe their nation had ever experienced. They were in exile because of generations of sin. They had lost everything. And into that darkness, God said: I'm not done with you. There is still a future. But the road to that future runs through patience, through prayer for your enemies, through decades of faithfulness in a place you never wanted to be.

The promise was real. But so was the cost of receiving it.

WHAT THIS MEANS FOR US

First, leadership matters more than we think. The kings of Judah led their nation to destruction through greed, injustice, and refusal to listen. Bad leadership doesn't just affect the leader. It pulls everyone else down with them. Josiah stands as the counterexample: a leader who knew God because he did justice and defended the poor. The quality of a leader is measured not by their power or their palace but by how they treat the people under their care.

Second, beware of people who only tell you what you want to hear. The false prophets were popular because they promised peace when there was no peace. Hananiah told the people the crisis would be over in two years, and they loved him for it. Jeremiah told them the truth, and they hated him. Comfortable lies are always more popular than uncomfortable truths. But comfortable lies will destroy you. Learn to value the people who tell you hard things, because they may be the only ones who actually care about your future.

Third, God's plans are real, but they don't skip over the hard parts. Jeremiah 29:11 is a genuine promise, but it came to people in the middle of exile, not people lounging in comfort. God's plans included seventy years of waiting, praying for enemies, and building new lives in a foreign land. Hope and hardship lived side by side. They still do.

Fourth, God can use anyone to accomplish his purposes, including people who don't know him. Nebuchadnezzar was called God's servant. That doesn't mean God approved of everything Babylon did. It means God's sovereignty extends even over the actions of pagan empires. Nothing is outside his control, even when everything looks out of control.

Fifth, knowing God is shown by how you live, not by what you claim. The false prophets claimed to speak for God. The kings claimed to serve God. But God pointed to Josiah and said, "That is what it means to know me." Faith that doesn't show up in the way you treat other people, especially the poor and powerless, isn't the kind of faith God recognizes.

TALKING POINTS

1. **God said that Josiah knew him because Josiah "did what was right and just" and "defended the cause of the poor and needy."** How does that definition of knowing God

compare to how most people think about it? What would it look like in your own life to know God in the way Josiah did?

2. **The false prophets told people "Peace, peace" when there was no peace.** Why is it so tempting to believe comfortable lies rather than hard truths? How can you learn to recognize when someone is telling you what you want to hear instead of what you need to hear?

3. **Hananiah publicly broke Jeremiah's yoke and predicted the crisis would end in two years. Jeremiah walked away without arguing and waited for God to speak.** What does Jeremiah's response teach about how to handle disagreements, especially when you're confident you're right?

4. **God told the exiles to "seek the peace and prosperity" of Babylon, the city of their captors.** Why would God ask his people to pray for their enemies? What might change in your own life if you started praying for people you don't get along with?

5. **Jeremiah 29:11 is one of the most quoted verses in the Bible.** How does knowing its original context, a letter to devastated exiles facing decades in a foreign land, change the way you understand that promise? Does it make it more meaningful or less?

The kings had been exposed. The false prophets had been unmasked. A letter had been sent to the exiles offering them the most unexpected gift: a future. But Jeremiah still had more to say. In the chapters ahead, the tone would shift from judgment to something the readers of this book have been waiting for since page one. Hope. Real, detailed, breathtaking hope. The kind that could survive even the ruins of Jerusalem.

Turn the page.

6

THE PROMISE OF SOMETHING NEW

Near the end of the movie *It's a Wonderful Life*, a man named George Bailey stands on a bridge in a snowstorm, ready to end his life. Everything he built has fallen apart. His business is collapsing. He's about to be arrested. He believes his family would be better off without him. From where George is standing, the future is nothing but darkness.

Then something extraordinary happens. An angel shows George what the world would look like if he had never been born. His town is ruined. People he loved are broken. Lives he saved were never saved. The community he held together has come undone. George sees a world without hope, and it terrifies him.

And then he's back on the bridge. Alive. The snow falling on his face. His hands shaking. And he runs. He runs through the streets of his little town shouting like a man set free from prison. He bursts through his front door and grabs his children. His neighbors flood into his house. Money pours onto the table. People who had been touched by his life show up to carry him through the crisis. The man who thought the story was over discovers that the best part was still being written.

That feeling, the overwhelming flood of joy when you realize that what looked like the end was actually the beginning of something new, is exactly what fills Jeremiah 30–33.

For twenty-nine chapters, we have been reading one of the darkest, most grief-soaked sections of the Bible. Broken covenants, broken hearts, a nation racing toward destruction, a prophet weeping himself dry. If the book of Jeremiah were George Bailey's story, we've been standing on the bridge in the dark, staring into the water, convinced the future is gone.

But now the angel shows up. And everything changes.

THE BOOK OF CONSOLATION

Scholars call Jeremiah 30–33 the "Book of Consolation" because these four chapters are almost entirely devoted to comfort, promise, and hope. After chapter upon chapter of warning and grief, the tone shifts so dramatically it almost feels like a different book. Colors that had been drained from the landscape come flooding back. Music that had been silenced starts playing again. The God who had been declaring judgment now declares restoration.

But this isn't cheap hope. This isn't God pretending the bad things didn't happen or sweeping the people's sin under a rug. Every promise in these chapters is spoken against the backdrop of real devastation. The exile happened. The temple was destroyed. People died. Families were torn apart. God's judgment was real, and it was deserved.

What makes these chapters so powerful is that the hope they offer comes after the worst has already happened, not instead of it. This is hope for people sitting in the rubble, not people trying to avoid it.

THE GREAT REVERSAL

One of the most remarkable things about the Book of Consolation is how deliberately it reverses the language of judgment from earlier in the book. Again and again, a phrase that once announced destruction is now reused to announce restoration.

Earlier, Jeremiah described a wound with no cure. Now God says, "I will restore you to health and heal your wounds."

Earlier, all the sounds of joy, the voices of the bride and groom, the laughter at weddings, had been silenced by judgment. Now God promises those sounds will return: "There will be heard once more the sounds of joy and gladness, the voices of bride and bridegroom."

Earlier, God told Jeremiah to stop praying because he would not listen. Now he promises a restored relationship where his people will call on him and he will answer.

Earlier, the land of the north was the source of terrifying invasion. Now that same direction becomes the source of returning exiles coming home.

It's as if God took every sentence of judgment he had spoken through Jeremiah and wrote a matching sentence of grace to go alongside it. The darkness doesn't disappear. But light breaks through it, point by point, sorrow by sorrow, promise by promise.

LOVED WITH AN EVERLASTING LOVE

The emotional heart of these chapters comes in a single verse that has echoed through centuries of worship and prayer: "I have loved you with an everlasting love; I have drawn you with unfailing kindness."

Remember what God said back in chapter 2? He remembered the honeymoon, the early days when Israel loved him like a bride and followed him into the wilderness. That love had been betrayed. The bride had wandered after other gods. The marriage had fallen apart.

But God's love never stopped. Even through the judgment, even through the exile, even through the years of silence and suffering, the love that began before the exodus was still burning. Not because Israel deserved it. They had done nothing to earn it and everything to forfeit it. But God's love wasn't a response to their goodness. It was an expression of his character. It was everlasting because he is everlasting.

And so God addresses ruined, exiled, shame-covered Israel with a word that would have taken their breath away: "I will build you up again, and you, Virgin Israel, will be rebuilt." The unfaithful wife is called a virgin. The broken nation is called a bride. God isn't just forgiving the past. He's creating something so new that it's as if the past didn't define them anymore.

RACHEL WEEPING

In the middle of all this hope, one of the most haunting images in the Bible appears. "A voice is heard in Ramah, mourning and great weeping. Rachel is weeping for her children and refusing to be comforted, because they are no more."

Rachel, the ancestor of Israel, is pictured crying over the loss of her descendants. She represents every mother who watched her children being marched away into exile or killed in the fall of Jerusalem. Her grief is bottomless. She refuses comfort because there is no comfort adequate to what she has lost.

But God speaks directly to her: "Restrain your voice from weeping and your eyes from tears, for your work will be rewarded. They will return from the land of the enemy. So there is hope for your descendants."

Centuries later, Matthew quoted this passage when Herod slaughtered the children of Bethlehem after Jesus was born. Even that unspeakable tragedy existed within a larger story where God's promise of restoration was still unfolding. The grief was real. The hope was also real. And the hope would ultimately outlast the grief.

THE NEW COVENANT

Then comes the passage that changes everything. Not just for Israel. For the entire Bible. "The days are coming," declares the Lord, "when I will make a new covenant with the people of Israel and with the people of Judah. It will not be like the covenant I made with their ancestors when I took them by the hand to lead them out of Egypt, because they broke my covenant, though I was a husband to them."

God is announcing the end of an era and the beginning of another. The old covenant, the one made at Mount Sinai after the exodus, was good. It was given by God. It revealed his character and his will. But the people had broken it, repeatedly and catastrophically. The entire first half of Jeremiah is the evidence. No matter how many times God called them back, no matter how many prophets he sent, the people could not or would not keep the covenant. The problem wasn't with the law. The problem was with the human heart.

So God promised to address the problem at its root. "I will put my law in their minds and write it on their hearts. I will be their God, and they will be my people. No longer will they teach their neighbor, or say to one another, 'Know the Lord,' because they will all know me, from the least of them to the greatest. For I will forgive their wickedness and will remember their sins no more."

Four promises are packed into this passage, and each one is staggering.

First, God would put his law inside his people rather than just in front of them. The old covenant was written on stone tablets. The new covenant would be written on hearts. Obedience would come from within, not just as a response to an external command, but as an impulse planted by God himself.

Second, the covenant relationship itself, "I will be their God and they will be my people," would continue. This was not a rejection of the old relationship but a transformation of it. The same God who had chosen Israel from the beginning was choosing them again, on new terms.

Third, knowledge of God would become universal among his people. Not just the priests, not just the scholars, not just the elite. Everyone, from the least to the greatest, would know him. And "knowing God" in Jeremiah's vocabulary, as we saw with Josiah, meant living justly and caring for the poor, not just having correct theological information.

Fourth, and this is the foundation of everything else, God would forgive their sins completely. "I will remember their sins no more." The guilt that had piled up for centuries, the guilt that made the exile necessary, the guilt that seemed to make any future relationship with God impossible, would be dealt with permanently. Not swept aside. Not minimized. Forgiven. Finished. Gone.

This is the passage that the New Testament quotes more than any other from Jeremiah. When Jesus held up the cup at the Last Supper and said, "This cup is the new covenant in my blood," he was pointing back to these very words. The writer of Hebrews quoted the entire passage to explain what Jesus accomplished through his death and resurrection. The new covenant that Jeremiah promised found its fulfillment in Christ.

BUYING A FIELD IN A WAR ZONE

If the new covenant passage is the theological peak of the Book of Consolation, then chapter 32 is its most dramatic scene.

Jerusalem was under siege. Babylonian armies surrounded the city. Famine was setting in. People were dying. Jeremiah himself was locked up in the courtyard of the royal guard, imprisoned by a king who didn't want to hear his message.

And in the middle of all that, God told Jeremiah to buy a field.

His cousin Hanamel showed up with a real estate proposition: buy a piece of family land near their village of Anathoth. Under normal circumstances, this would have been a reasonable act of family loyalty. But these were not normal circumstances. The land was almost certainly being trampled by Babylonian soldiers. The village was likely destroyed. Jeremiah had no wife, no children, and no guarantee he would ever leave prison alive. Buying a field at that moment was like buying a ticket to a concert during an earthquake.

But Jeremiah did it. He paid seventeen shekels of silver. He signed the deed. He had Baruch witness and seal the documents and store them in a clay jar "so they will last a long time." And then he declared God's message: "Houses, fields and vineyards will again be bought in this land."

It was an act of faith so audacious it's almost funny. Everything visible said the future was over. The siege engines, the starvation, the smoke, the armies, all of it pointed to one conclusion: this nation is finished. And Jeremiah, sitting in a military prison with the walls literally crumbling around him, invested in real estate.

Why? Because God had said there would be a future. And Jeremiah believed him. Not because the evidence supported it. The evidence pointed in exactly the opposite direction. He believed because God had spoken, and God's word was more real to him than Babylonian siege ramps.

After the purchase, Jeremiah prayed, "Lord, you are the God who made everything, and nothing is too hard for you. But... you just told me to buy a field while the city is falling. Help me understand." God's answer was simple and staggering: yes, the city would fall. Yes, the judgment was real. But "I will surely gather them from all the lands where I banish them... I will bring them back to this place and let them live in safety. They will be my people, and I will be their God."

Judgment and hope. Wrath and mercy. Both real, both from the same God, both at the same time.

AS PERMANENT AS THE STARS

God knew the exiles would have one nagging fear: What if this happens again? What if we come back and then blow it all over again and God scatters us for good?

So God anchored his promises in the most permanent things the human eye can see. "This is what the Lord says, he who appoints the sun to shine by day, who decrees the moon and stars to shine by night, who stirs up the sea so that its waves roar: Only if these decrees vanish from my sight will the descendants of Israel ever cease to be a nation before me."

In other words, as long as the sun comes up tomorrow, God's commitment to his people stands. As long as the stars shine at night, Israel has a future. The God who made the universe and keeps it running is the same God who made this promise, and his word is as reliable as the sunrise.

WHAT THIS MEANS FOR US

First, God's love is not a response to our performance. Israel had done nothing to deserve the promises in these chapters. They had broken the covenant, ignored the prophets, and earned every ounce of judgment they received. And God loved them anyway. Not because of who they were, but because of who he is. That kind of love can't be earned, and it can't be lost through failure. It can only be received.

Second, the new covenant means God fixes what we can't fix ourselves. The problem with the old covenant was never the law itself. It was the human heart. People couldn't keep the covenant because their hearts were hardened by sin. So God promised to change the heart from the inside out. That's the gospel. God doesn't just give us rules and hope we follow them. He gives us new hearts and the power to live differently.

Third, real faith acts before the evidence arrives. Jeremiah bought a field in the middle of a siege. He didn't wait until the war was over and the economy recovered. He put his money down when everything looked hopeless. That's what faith does. It acts on what God has said, even when what you can see tells a different story.

Fourth, hope doesn't erase the pain; it outlasts it. Rachel wept for her children, and her grief was real. The exile was real. The suffering was real. God didn't wave it away. But he spoke a promise that reached beyond the grief to a future where the tears would stop and the children would come home. Sometimes hope doesn't mean the pain goes away. It means there's something on the other side of it.

Fifth, God's promises are as permanent as creation itself. If you've ever wondered whether God might give up on his people, look at the sky tonight. The stars are still there. And so is his commitment.

TALKING POINTS

1. **God reversed almost every judgment statement from earlier in the book with a matching promise of restoration.** What does that tell you about how God thinks about judgment? Is judgment always his final word, or is there something beyond it?

2. **The new covenant promised that God would put his law "in their minds and write it on their hearts."** What's the difference between obeying a rule because it's written on a

stone tablet in front of you and obeying it because it's been written on your heart? What does internal obedience look like in everyday life?

3. **Jeremiah bought a field in the middle of a siege.** Has there ever been a time when you had to act on something you believed was true, even though the circumstances seemed to say the opposite? What made it hard? What made it possible?

4. **God told the exiles that his commitment to them was as permanent as the sun and the stars.** Why do you think God used creation itself as the measure of his faithfulness? What does that comparison tell you about how seriously God takes his promises?

5. **Rachel's weeping is quoted again in Matthew's Gospel when Herod kills the children of Bethlehem.** How can a passage about deep grief also be a passage about hope? Is it possible for grief and hope to exist in the same moment?

The angel had shown up. After all the dark chapters, all the warnings, all the tears, God had revealed what was on the other side of judgment: a new covenant, a new heart, a new beginning. But the siege wasn't over yet. The city still had to fall. And when it did, Jeremiah would be there to witness it.

Turn the page.

7

THE CITY FALLS

You know that feeling when a big storm is coming? The sky turns a strange color. The wind picks up. The air feels heavy and electric. Your phone buzzes with weather alerts. Your parents start moving things inside, closing windows, checking flashlights. And there's this stretch of time—maybe an hour, maybe less—where you know the storm is going to hit but it hasn't arrived yet. You can see the dark wall of clouds on the horizon, crawling closer and closer. Everything gets quiet in that eerie way it does right before the worst of it. All you can do is wait.

Then it hits. And no matter how much you prepared, no matter how many warnings you received, the force of it still takes your breath away.

That's what Jeremiah 34–39 feels like. The storm has been building for the entire book. For chapters and chapters, the clouds have been gathering, the warnings have been sounding, the sky has been darkening. Now the wind hits. These chapters tell the story of the last days of Jerusalem, and they include the most dramatic scenes in the entire book: a king who cuts up God's word and feeds it to a fire, a prophet thrown into a pit to die, an unexpected rescue by a foreign official, and the moment the walls of Jerusalem finally break.

This is where everything Jeremiah predicted comes true. And it is devastating.

A PROMISE BROKEN BEFORE THE INK DRIED

Chapter 34 gives us one final, bitter example of the kind of people Jerusalem's leaders had become. As the Babylonian army closed in, King Zedekiah had an idea. He made a covenant with the wealthy citizens of Jerusalem: they would free all their Hebrew slaves, as God's law had always required but they had always ignored.

For a brief moment, it worked. The slaves were released. Maybe it was genuine repentance. Maybe it was superstition, hoping that a last-minute act of obedience would convince God to save the city. Maybe it was a military calculation, trying to get more soldiers for the defense.

Whatever the reason, it didn't last. When the Babylonian army temporarily withdrew to deal with an Egyptian threat, the danger seemed to pass. And the slave-owners immediately grabbed their freed slaves and forced them back into service.

God's response was furious. He reminded them that when he rescued Israel from slavery in Egypt, the very first laws he gave them included provisions for releasing slaves. The whole identity of Israel was built on the fact that God had set them free. For them to enslave their own brothers and sisters, release them under pressure, and then re-enslave them the moment the pressure lifted was a mockery of everything God had done for them.

"You have not obeyed me," God said. "You have not proclaimed freedom to your own people. So now I proclaim 'freedom' for you: freedom to fall by the sword, plague, and famine."

The chapter reads like a courtroom verdict. The nation had been offered its final chance to show that it understood what the covenant meant. It failed the test in less time than it took the Babylonian army to regroup.

THE SCROLL IN THE FIRE

Chapter 36 jumps back in time to an earlier reign, the rule of King Jehoiakim, to show us the moment when the nation's fate was truly sealed.

God told Jeremiah to take everything he had preached over the past twenty-three years and have it written on a scroll. Baruch, Jeremiah's faithful secretary, did the painstaking work of writing it all down as Jeremiah dictated. It took months. When it was finished, Baruch took the scroll to the temple on a day of public fasting and read it aloud to the crowds.

The scroll made its way through the levels of government. Mid-level officials heard it and were alarmed. "We must report this to the king," they said. But they also told Baruch to take Jeremiah and hide. They knew their king.

When the scroll was read to Jehoiakim, he was sitting in his winter apartment with a fire burning nearby. As the reader finished every three or four columns, the king took a knife, sliced off the section that had just been read, and dropped it into the fire. Column by column. Slowly. Deliberately. Until the entire scroll was ash.

Some of his officials begged him to stop. He ignored them.

This wasn't a fit of rage. It was a calculated, public act of contempt. Jehoiakim listened to every word God had spoken through Jeremiah over two decades, and then systematically destroyed it. He wasn't just rejecting a prophet. He was rejecting God's word itself, with a knife and a flame.

But God's word can't be burned. God told Jeremiah to have Baruch write the whole thing again. The second scroll was even longer than the first. And God added a personal message for Jehoiakim: because he had burned the scroll, his body would be thrown out unburied, exposed to the heat of day and the frost of night. The king who thought he could silence God's word with a knife discovered that the word outlasts every fire and every king who tries to destroy it.

INTO THE PIT

The story moves forward to the final siege under King Zedekiah. Jeremiah had been telling anyone who would listen that the only way to survive was to surrender to Babylon. To the government, this sounded like treason. When Jeremiah tried to leave the city during a temporary break in the siege, he was arrested at the gate, accused of defecting to the enemy, beaten, and thrown into an underground dungeon.

Zedekiah secretly sent for him and asked, "Is there any word from the Lord?" Jeremiah's answer was: "You will be handed over to the king of Babylon." Even from a dungeon, the message didn't change. Then Jeremiah made a personal appeal: "Don't send me back to that prison. I'll die there." Zedekiah moved him to the courtyard of the guard, where he at least received bread each day.

But the officials weren't satisfied. Jeremiah was still telling people to surrender, and in their minds, he was destroying the morale of the soldiers defending the city. They went to the king and demanded his death. Zedekiah's response revealed the full tragedy of his character: "He is in your hands. The king can do nothing to oppose you."

The king of Judah just admitted he was powerless to stop his own officials from killing God's prophet. Zedekiah knew Jeremiah spoke the truth. He kept summoning him in secret to hear God's word. But he was too afraid of his own court to act on it. He was a man with access to the truth and no courage to follow it.

The officials took Jeremiah and lowered him by ropes into an empty cistern, a deep underground water storage pit that had gone dry. He sank into the mud at the bottom. Without food or water, in the dark, stuck in the muck, he was left to die a slow death. The officials could tell themselves they hadn't technically killed him. They had just put him somewhere he couldn't survive.

THE MAN WHO CLIMBED DOWN

This is where one of the most unexpected heroes in the entire Bible shows up. His name was Ebed-Melek, and he was a foreigner. He was from Cush, a kingdom in Africa south of Egypt, and he served as an official in the royal palace. When he heard what had been done to Jeremiah, he went straight to the king, who was sitting at the Benjamin Gate, and said, "My lord the king, these men have acted wickedly in all they have done to Jeremiah the prophet. They have thrown him into a cistern, where he will starve to death."

The king authorized a rescue. Ebed-Melek gathered thirty men and a pile of old rags and worn-out clothes. He went to the cistern, lowered the rags down to Jeremiah, and told him to put them under his arms so the ropes wouldn't cut into his skin as they pulled him up. It's a small detail, but it reveals an extraordinary tenderness. In the middle of a city under siege, with people dying of starvation and the world collapsing around them, this man took the time to make sure the ropes wouldn't hurt the prophet's armpits.

Ebed-Melek pulled Jeremiah out of the mud and back into the light. And later, God sent a personal message to this African official through Jeremiah: "I will save you. You will not be given into the hands of those you fear. I will rescue you because you trust in me."

In a book filled with leaders who failed, prophets who lied, kings who refused to listen, and an entire nation that turned its back on God, a foreign servant in the palace became the hero of the story. Not because he was powerful. Because he was brave. And because he trusted in the God of Israel when the people of Israel wouldn't.

THE LAST CONVERSATION

Zedekiah summoned Jeremiah one final time for a secret meeting. Jeremiah gave him one last chance to make the right choice. "If you surrender to Babylon's officers, your life will be spared and this city will not be burned down. But if you do not, this city will be burned and you will not escape."

Zedekiah hesitated. He was afraid that the Judeans who had already defected might mistreat him. Jeremiah pushed harder: "Obey the Lord by doing what I tell you. Then it will go well with you, and your life will be spared."

Zedekiah chose nothing. He ended the conversation by telling Jeremiah to keep their meeting a secret. No decision was the decision. And it was the worst one he could have made.

THE WALLS COME DOWN

Chapter 39 tells the end in cold, factual language. The siege lasted eighteen months. In July of 587 BC, the walls were breached. The Babylonian commanders set up headquarters in the middle gate of the city. Zedekiah and his soldiers fled by night, running east toward the Jordan Valley. They were caught on the plains of Jericho.

Nebuchadnezzar dealt with Zedekiah at his headquarters in Riblah, far to the north. The last thing Zedekiah saw before his eyes were put out was the execution of his own sons. Then he was bound in chains and taken to Babylon, where he would die in prison.

A month later, Nebuchadnezzar's chief officer returned to Jerusalem and burned it. The temple. The palace. The houses. The walls were torn down. Most of the surviving population was marched into exile. Only the poorest people in the land were left behind and given vineyards and fields to tend.

The narrative is so restrained it's almost silent. After thirty-eight chapters of passionate poetry, gut-wrenching laments, and thundering prophecies, the actual fall of Jerusalem is reported in a handful of verses. No commentary. No theological explanation. No prophetic outburst. Just the facts.

Perhaps that's because everything that needed to be said had already been said. Or perhaps it's because the moment was so terrible that even the text falls quiet, the way people sometimes go silent in the presence of grief too deep for words.

But two details pierce through the silence. First, Jeremiah was freed. Nebuchadnezzar himself had given orders to find Jeremiah and treat him well. The Babylonians knew about the prophet who had been telling Judah to submit, and they made sure he was protected. Second, Ebed-Melek was saved, just as God had promised. In the middle of a catastrophe that swallowed a nation, God kept his word to one faithful foreigner who had trusted him.

WHAT THIS MEANS FOR US

First, you can destroy the paper, but you can't destroy the word. Jehoiakim burned every column of God's message, and Baruch wrote it again, longer than before. People have been trying to silence, ban, burn, and bury the Bible for thousands of years. It's still here. God's word outlasts every attempt to destroy it.

Second, courage sometimes looks like one person standing up when everyone else sits down. Ebed-Melek didn't have an army. He wasn't a priest or a prophet. He was a foreign official who saw injustice and refused to be silent. Sometimes the most important thing you can do is speak up for someone who can't speak for themselves, even when it's risky.

Third, knowing the truth is not the same as acting on it. Zedekiah believed Jeremiah. He kept seeking him out in secret. But he never found the courage to obey. The gap between knowing what's right and doing what's right is where most disasters happen. Faith that stays in your head and never reaches your hands is not faith at all.

Fourth, indecision is a decision. Zedekiah thought he could avoid choosing by not choosing. But refusing to decide was itself a choice, and it led to the worst possible outcome for himself, his family, and his entire nation. When God puts a choice in front of you, silence isn't neutral. It's an answer.

Fifth, God keeps his promises, even when the world is falling apart. In the middle of Jerusalem's destruction, God saved Jeremiah and Ebed-Melek. The city burned. The nation collapsed. But the two people who had trusted God were rescued. God's faithfulness doesn't depend on the stability of the world around you. It depends on the character of God.

TALKING POINTS

1. **The slave-owners freed their slaves and then re-enslaved them as soon as the pressure eased.** Why do you think people find it so easy to go back on promises they made during a crisis? What does that pattern reveal about human nature?

2. **Jehoiakim burned the scroll of God's word column by column.** What are some ways people today reject or ignore God's word, even if they don't literally burn it? Why is deliberate rejection more serious than simple ignorance?

3. **Ebed-Melek was a foreigner who showed more courage and faith than most of the Israelites in the story.** What does his example teach about who God uses and how faith shows up in unexpected places? Have you ever been surprised by who turned out to be the bravest person in a difficult situation?

4. Zedekiah kept meeting with Jeremiah in secret but never acted on what he heard. What's the danger of treating truth as something to think about privately rather than something to obey publicly? Can you think of times when you knew the right thing to do but hesitated to act?

5. **The fall of Jerusalem is described in just a few short verses, almost in silence.** Why do you think the text handles such a massive event so quietly? What does restraint in storytelling sometimes communicate that dramatic language cannot?

Jerusalem was gone. The temple was ash. The king was blind and in chains. Everything Jeremiah had warned about for forty years had come to pass. But the story wasn't over. A small, frightened group of survivors still huddled in the ruins, and they had one more decision to make. Jeremiah would have something to say about it.

Turn the page.

8

AFTER THE ASHES

George Orwell's *Animal Farm* tells the story of a group of farm animals who overthrow their cruel owner and take control of the farm themselves. At first, everything is hopeful. The animals write their own rules. They work their own land. They govern themselves. Freedom tastes incredible after years of being exploited.

But slowly, things start to go wrong. The pigs, who appointed themselves leaders, begin making exceptions to the rules. They sleep in the farmer's bed. They drink his whiskey. They walk on two legs. And by the final page of the book, the other animals look through the farmhouse window at the pigs sitting at the table with human farmers, and they cannot tell the difference between the pigs and the men. The animals who fought so hard for freedom have become exactly what they were freed from.

That story could have been written about the survivors of Jerusalem. Because in Jeremiah 40–45, the last remnant of God's people, the descendants of slaves who were liberated from Egypt in the greatest rescue operation in the Old Testament, voluntarily walk back to Egypt. They undo their own exodus. They return to the house of slavery their ancestors escaped centuries earlier, and they do it by choice.

This is the final act of Jeremiah's story, and it might be the saddest part of the whole book.

A FLICKER OF HOPE

After the destruction of Jerusalem, the Babylonians appointed a man named Gedaliah to govern the survivors who remained in the land. Gedaliah was the grandson of Shaphan, a member of the family that had supported Josiah's reforms and protected Jeremiah more than once. He was, by all appearances, exactly the kind of leader the shattered remnant of Judah needed.

Gedaliah set up his headquarters at Mizpah, a small town north of the ruined capital. Survivors began trickling in from hiding places in the hills and from the surrounding countries where they had fled during the invasion. Armed groups came in from the countryside and submitted to his authority. Gedaliah gave them a speech that echoed the words Jeremiah had sent to the exiles in Babylon: settle down, serve the king of Babylon, farm the land, and it will go well with you. Don't be afraid.

And it worked. For a brief season, the remnant of Judah gathered around this good leader, harvested the crops in the fields, and began to piece together some kind of life in the ruins. Jeremiah himself joined the community at Mizpah, choosing to stay with the struggling survivors rather than accept the Babylonians' offer of comfortable treatment in Babylon.

It was a small, fragile flicker of hope. And it was about to be snuffed out.

THE ASSASSINATION

A man named Ishmael, a member of the royal family, had been watching Gedaliah's rise with bitter resentment. Ishmael was a nationalist, an angry man who saw Gedaliah's cooperation with Babylon as treason against the fallen kingdom. Backed by the king of Ammon across the Jordan, Ishmael hatched a plot.

Gedaliah was warned. One of his officers, Johanan, told him directly: Ishmael is planning to kill you. Gedaliah didn't believe it. He may have been wise and good, but he was also fatally trusting. He invited Ishmael to dinner.

Ishmael came to the meal at Mizpah with ten men. In the middle of the feast, they rose and murdered Gedaliah, along with the Judean officials and the Babylonian soldiers stationed there. The next day, before anyone knew what had happened, Ishmael intercepted a group of eighty men traveling to worship at the ruins of the temple and slaughtered most of them. Then he took the rest of the people at Mizpah hostage, including women, children, and royal daughters, and started marching them east toward Ammon.

Johanan gathered a fighting force and intercepted Ishmael near Gibeon. The hostages were rescued, but Ishmael and eight of his men escaped across the border. The rescue was a relief, but the damage was catastrophic. Gedaliah was dead. The one leader who could have held the remnant together was gone. The community that had started to rebuild was shattered. And now they faced a terrifying new problem: when the Babylonians learned that their appointed governor had been assassinated, they would come back. And their response would not be gentle.

THE QUESTION THEY ALREADY KNEW THE ANSWER TO

Johanan and the other leaders gathered the frightened survivors and turned south, heading toward Egypt. But before they left the land, they stopped and did something that, on the surface, looked commendable. They went to Jeremiah and asked for God's guidance.

"Please hear our petition," they said. "Pray to the Lord your God for this entire remnant. Tell us where we should go and what we should do."

Jeremiah agreed. And the people made a solemn promise: "Whether it is favorable or unfavorable, we will obey the Lord our God, to whom we are sending you, so that it will go well with us."

It sounded sincere. But there was a problem. They were already packed. They were already heading south. The question about where to go had, for most of them, already been answered in their hearts before they ever opened their mouths. They didn't want guidance. They wanted confirmation.

GOD'S ANSWER

Ten days passed before God's word came to Jeremiah. When it did, the answer was clear, detailed, and everything the people did not want to hear.

"If you stay in this land, I will build you up and not tear you down; I will plant you and not uproot you, for I relent concerning the disaster I have inflicted on you. Do not be afraid of the king of Babylon, whom you now fear. Do not be afraid of him, for I am with you and will save you and deliver you from his hands. I will show you compassion, so that he will have compassion on you and restore you to your land."

Those words are some of the most tender in the entire book. After forty years of warning, judgment, and tears, God was offering this tiny, terrified group the same language he had used when he first called Jeremiah: "I will build you up. I will plant you. Do not be afraid. I am with you." The very words that had defined the beginning of Jeremiah's ministry were being offered now, at the end of it, to the ragged survivors of the catastrophe that ministry had predicted.

But God didn't stop there. He also laid out what would happen if they chose Egypt instead. The sword and famine they feared in Judah would follow them to Egypt. They would die there. They would never see the land again. Egypt would not be an escape. It would be a dead end.

The alternatives were stark. Stay and trust God, with his promise of protection. Or run to Egypt and face exactly the fate you were trying to avoid.

THE EXODUS IN REVERSE

The people's response was as predictable as it was heartbreaking. They accused Jeremiah of lying. They said Baruch had manipulated him. And they did the one thing God had told them not to do.

They went to Egypt.

And they took Jeremiah with them. The prophet who had spent his entire life speaking God's word to a people who wouldn't listen was now physically dragged into a foreign country by the very people he was trying to save. He had been freed from Babylonian chains only to be carried into Egyptian exile by his own countrymen.

The biblical writer wants you to feel the weight of what just happened. This wasn't just a group of refugees making a practical decision about safety. This was the story of Israel running backward. God had brought their ancestors out of Egypt centuries earlier in the greatest act of salvation the Old Testament records. The entire identity of Israel was built on the exodus: "I am the Lord your God, who brought you out of the land of Egypt, out of the house of slavery."

And now, the last surviving fragment of that nation was voluntarily walking back into Egypt. The exodus was being undone. The promised land was behind them. The house of slavery was ahead. Everything God had done to bring Israel out, this remnant was reversing by walking back in.

THE QUEEN OF HEAVEN

Once settled in Egypt, the survivors didn't just fail to worship God. They actively and defiantly worshiped other gods. When Jeremiah confronted them about burning incense to the "Queen of Heaven," a foreign goddess, the people's response was breathtaking in its stubbornness.

"We will not listen to you," they said. "We will certainly do everything we said we would: we will burn incense to the Queen of Heaven and pour out drink offerings to her just as we and our ancestors, our kings and our officials did in the towns of Judah and in the streets of Jerusalem. At that time we had plenty of food and were well off and suffered no harm. But ever since we stopped burning incense to the Queen of Heaven, we have had nothing but trouble."

Read that carefully. They looked at the same history

Jeremiah had been interpreting for four decades and drew the exact opposite conclusion. Jeremiah said their troubles came from abandoning God. They said their troubles came from abandoning the Queen of Heaven. When Josiah had reformed the nation's worship and removed the foreign idols, these people believed that was when things started going wrong. In their minds, faithfulness to God was the problem, and idolatry was the solution.

It's a staggering example of how people can look at the same set of facts and construct completely opposite stories about what they mean. The human capacity for self-deception, even in the face of overwhelming evidence, has no limits.

Jeremiah gave them one final word from God. Because they had chosen to reject the God who had rescued their ancestors from this very land, God would withdraw his name from them. They would no longer be able to call themselves his people. The few who survived would eventually return to Judah, but the community in Egypt as a whole had written itself out of the story.

A WORD FOR THE FAITHFUL FRIEND

The final chapter in this section, chapter 45, is one of the shortest and most personal passages in the book. It's addressed not to the nation, not to the kings, not to the false prophets, but to one man: Baruch.

Baruch had been at Jeremiah's side for years. He was the one who wrote down Jeremiah's words on the first scroll, the one who read it aloud in the temple at risk of his own life, the one who handled the legal paperwork when Jeremiah bought a field in the middle of a siege, and the one who was dragged to Egypt alongside his master. He was faithful, brave, and exhausted.

At some point during the long process of writing Jeremiah's prophecies, Baruch had broken down. "Woe to me!" he cried. "The Lord has added sorrow to my pain. I am worn out with groaning and find no rest."

God's response to Baruch was tender but direct. First, God acknowledged his own pain: "I am about to tear down what I have built and uproot what I have planted, throughout the earth." God was saying, "You think this is hard for you? I built this nation. I planted this people. And now I'm watching it all be torn apart. Your pain is real, but mine is greater than you can imagine."

Then God challenged Baruch's ambitions: "Should you then seek great things for yourself? Do not seek them." Whatever career plans, personal goals, or dreams of significance Baruch had been nurturing, God was telling him to let them go. The world was falling apart. This was not the time for self-advancement.

But God ended with a promise: "Wherever you go, I will let you escape with your life." It wasn't the promise of comfort or success. It was the promise of survival. In a world where nations were being crushed and kings were being blinded and everything stable was being swept away, God promised this one faithful man that he would live. Your life will be your prize, carried out of the wreckage like a trophy from a battlefield.

It's a small promise. But in the middle of a catastrophe, the promise of life is everything.

WHAT THIS MEANS FOR US

First, asking for God's guidance only counts if you're willing

to follow it. The survivors went through every motion of seeking God's will: they approached the prophet, they made solemn vows, they waited ten days for the answer. But they had already decided what they were going to do. Seeking God's direction while secretly determined to go your own way isn't faith. It's performance.

Second, fear makes terrible decisions. The survivors were terrified of Babylon, and that fear drove them to Egypt against God's explicit command. Fear has a way of making the wrong choice look like the safe choice. God's path often looks more dangerous than the alternative, because God's path requires trust in something you can't see. But the "safe" choice that ignores God's word is never actually safe.

Third, you can rewrite history to justify anything. The people in Egypt looked at decades of national tragedy and concluded that their problem was too much faithfulness to God, not too little. If you're determined to believe something, you can always find a way to make the evidence fit. The only defense against this is a willingness to let God's word challenge your interpretation of your own experience.

Fourth, faithful service often goes unrecognized. Baruch spent his life serving Jeremiah and, through him, serving God. He wrote scrolls, handled legal documents, risked his life reading unpopular prophecies in public, and followed Jeremiah to the end. His reward was not fame or prosperity. It was survival. But without Baruch, we might not have the book of Jeremiah at all. The most important people in God's story are often the ones nobody remembers.

Fifth, God's pain is bigger than yours. When Baruch

groaned under the weight of his suffering, God didn't dismiss his feelings. But he did put them in perspective. God was watching his own creation, his own people, his own centuries-long project of redemption, being torn to pieces. Whatever you're carrying, God is carrying more. And he still shows up. He still speaks. He still promises life to those who trust him.

TALKING POINTS

1. **The survivors promised to obey God no matter what he said, and then immediately disobeyed when the answer wasn't what they wanted.** Why is it so hard to follow through on promises to obey God when obedience feels scary or inconvenient? Have you ever asked for advice you didn't actually want to follow?

2. **Going to Egypt was described as an "exodus in reverse," undoing God's greatest act of salvation.** What are some ways people today might "go back to Egypt," returning to old patterns, old habits, or old sources of false security that God has already rescued them from?

3. **The people in Egypt claimed that their troubles starteded when they stopped worshiping the Queen of Heaven.** How do people today rewrite their own history to justify choices they've already made? What makes it so hard to accept an interpretation of events that challenges what you want to believe?

4. **God told Baruch, "Should you then seek great things for yourself? Do not seek them."** What do you think God meant? Is ambition always wrong, or was there something specific about Baruch's situation that made personal ambition

inappropriate? How do you know when to pursue your goals and when to let them go?

5. **Baruch's reward for a lifetime of faithful service was simply: "I will let you escape with your life."** How does that compare to what most people expect as a reward for faithfulness? In what situations might the promise of survival be the most precious gift God could give?

Jeremiah's story with his own people ends here, in Egypt, among a community that refused to listen to the very last word he ever spoke to them. But the book of Jeremiah isn't finished. There is one more section to go: a sweeping collection of prophecies about the nations surrounding Israel, reminding us that the God who judged his own people is the God of the whole earth, and his purposes don't stop at the borders of one small country.

Turn the page.

9

GOD OVER ALL NATIONS

Have you ever been stuck in something that felt like it would never end? Maybe it was a school year with a teacher who made every day miserable. Maybe it was a season when your family was going through something hard and you couldn't see the other side of it. Maybe it was just a long, dark stretch when nothing seemed to be getting better, and you started to wonder if things would always be this way.

And then, one day, it ended. The school year finished. The hard season passed. You woke up and realized the thing you thought was permanent was actually temporary. It just hadn't felt that way while you were in the middle of it.

The people of Judah spent decades in exile. They watched their city burn, saw their king blinded and chained, and were marched a thousand miles to live as captives in a foreign land. Babylon seemed eternal. Its walls were massive. Its armies were unstoppable. Its gods were everywhere. For the exiles, it must have felt like Babylon would last forever and they would die there forgotten.

The final chapters of Jeremiah say otherwise. Chapters 46–52 zoom out from the story of Israel and sweep across the entire ancient world to make one massive point: the God of Israel is not just the God of Israel. He is the God of every nation on earth. Empires rise and fall at his word. No power, no matter how great, lasts forever. And at the very end of the book, in the last handful of verses, a prison door swings open, and the tiniest glimmer of hope breaks through.

A PROPHET TO THE NATIONS

When God first called Jeremiah as a teenager, he didn't just say, "I'm making you a prophet to Judah." He said, "I appoint you as a prophet over nations and kingdoms, to uproot and tear down, to destroy and overthrow, to build and to plant." Jeremiah's assignment was always bigger than one small country. And in these final chapters, that international scope comes fully into view.

Chapters 46–49 contain prophecies against nearly every nation in the region: Egypt, the Philistines, Moab, Ammon, Edom, Damascus, the Arabian tribes, and Elam far to the east. One by one, God addresses the nations surrounding Israel and delivers the same basic message: you are not outside my reach. Your pride, your violence, your false gods, your military power will not protect you. What I did to my own people, I will do to you.

These prophecies aren't random lists of threats. They carry a specific theological point. Throughout the book, people might have assumed that God's judgment on Israel was a local affair, a family dispute between one small nation and its particular God. These chapters shatter that assumption. The God who judged Judah is the same God who holds every nation accountable. The same moral standards apply everywhere.

Violence will be answered. Arrogance will be humbled. False gods will fail.

GOD WEEPS FOR HIS ENEMIES

But here's what makes these chapters truly remarkable. They aren't just speeches of judgment. Buried inside the oracle against Moab, one of Israel's oldest rivals, is a detail so startling it can stop you mid-sentence.

God weeps for Moab.

"Therefore I wail over Moab, for all Moab I cry out," God says. "My heart laments for Moab like the sound of a pipe." Three times in chapter 48, God expresses personal grief over the suffering of a nation that isn't even his covenant people. This is the same God who wept over Jerusalem through the tears of Jeremiah. Now he weeps over a foreign nation facing the same kind of devastation.

That changes everything about how we understand God's judgment. This is not a God who takes pleasure in destroying nations. This is a God who grieves over the suffering that human sin and pride make necessary. Even when judgment falls on people who have defied him, God mourns. The anger is real, but so are the tears.

And there's more. Several of these oracles end with a promise that God will "restore the fortunes" of the nation being judged. Moab, Ammon, Elam, and even Egypt are told that their destruction won't be the final word. The same language God used to promise restoration for Israel is extended, in smaller measure, to foreign nations. The God who promised a future for his own people also has plans for the rest of the world.

THE FALL OF BABYLON

Then comes the climax: two enormous chapters, 50–51, aimed at Babylon itself. These are the longest oracles in the entire book, and they carry the heaviest theological weight. Everything the book has been building toward arrives here.

For years, Jeremiah had told the people that Babylon was God's instrument of judgment. He called Nebuchadnezzar "my servant." He told the nations to submit to Babylonian rule. He told the exiles to settle down in Babylon, build houses, plant gardens, and pray for the city's welfare.

But none of that meant God approved of Babylon's character. Babylon had been used as a tool. Now the tool would be judged. And the charges were devastating.

Babylon was arrogant. They had set themselves up as masters of the world, answerable to no one. They trusted in their military power, their wealth, their gods, and their seemingly impenetrable walls. "You who live by many waters and are rich in treasures, your end has come," God said.

Babylon was violent. They had gone far beyond what any divine mandate required, inflicting cruelty and destruction on a massive scale. The retributive principle that runs through the whole Bible applies here: what you have done to others will be done to you.

And Babylon was idolatrous. Their gods were nothing but human constructions, and the whole imperial system was built on the worship of power, wealth, and military dominance. In the end, those gods would be as useless to Babylon as Baal had been to Israel.

The language describing Babylon's fall is enormous. Armies from the north. Cities burned. Walls shattered. A land left desolate. Much of this language is poetic and symbolic, painting a picture of total, permanent collapse rather than giving a play-by-play military account. When Babylon did fall to the Persian king Cyrus in 539 BC, it actually happened with very little fighting. But the point of the prophecy was never the method of the fall. It was the certainty of it. Babylon will fall. Period. No empire lasts forever. No human power is permanent. Only the kingdom of God endures.

And woven through these chapters of judgment against Babylon is the matching promise of redemption for Israel. Every time the text declares that Babylon will be destroyed, it also declares that Israel will be restored. The two themes are inseparable. God's judgment on the oppressor is God's salvation for the oppressed. The fall of Babylon is the exodus of the exiles.

"In those days, at that time," God declares, "the people of Israel and the people of Judah together will go in tears to seek the Lord their God. They will ask the way to Zion and turn their faces toward it. They will come and bind themselves to the Lord in an everlasting covenant that will not be forgotten."

There it is again: the new covenant. The promise from chapter 31. The whole arc of the book comes together in these final pages. Judgment and hope. The fall of the empire and the restoration of the people. The end of exile and the beginning of something new.

THE SCROLL IN THE RIVER

One of the most dramatic moments in the book happens quietly at the end of chapter 51. Years earlier, when Zedekiah was still king, Jeremiah had written his prophecies against Babylon on a scroll and given it to Baruch's brother Seraiah, who was traveling to Babylon on a diplomatic mission.

Jeremiah's instructions were specific. When you get to Babylon, read this scroll aloud. Then tie a stone to it and throw it into the Euphrates River. As it sinks, say these words: "So will Babylon sink to rise no more, because of the disaster I will bring on her."

Picture that scene. A man standing on the banks of the greatest river in the world's greatest empire, watching a scroll disappear beneath the water. No armies in sight. No walls crumbling. Just a man, a stone, a scroll, and a river. And a promise from God that everything this empire had built would one day sink just as surely as that scroll.

The chapter closes with a single sentence: "The words of Jeremiah end here."

ONE LAST SCENE

But the book doesn't end there. Chapter 52 is an appendix, added by the editors who compiled Jeremiah's writings. It retells the fall of Jerusalem one more time, in cold, factual language borrowed almost word for word from 2 Kings. The siege. The breach. The capture of Zedekiah. The burning of the temple. The looting. The deportations. Everything Jeremiah had predicted for forty years, laid out in a simple historical record. The word of the Lord, confirmed by the facts of history.

Then comes the very last paragraph. And it changes everything.

Thirty-seven years after being taken to Babylon as a

prisoner, the exiled king Jehoiachin was released from prison. The new king of Babylon lifted him up, spoke kindly to him, gave him a seat of honor above the other captive kings, and provided for him for the rest of his life.

That's how the book of Jeremiah ends. Not with the roaring fall of Babylon. Not with a triumphant return from exile. Not with a rebuilt temple or a new king on the throne. It ends with a small, quiet act of kindness toward a broken old man in a foreign land.

Why does it matter? Because Jehoiachin was a descendant of David. He represented the royal line that God had promised would never be completely cut off. And his release from prison, small as it was, was a sign. If God could show grace to the exiled king, then the exile itself was not the end of the story. If a prison door could open for Jehoiachin, then the doors of Babylon could open for all the exiles.

It was barely a whisper of hope. But it was real. And for people who had been listening to Jeremiah's promises about a future and a hope, about a new covenant and a righteous Branch from David's line, that whisper was enough to keep believing.

Centuries later, a descendant of Jehoiachin would be born in Bethlehem. His name would be Jesus. And he would fulfill every promise the book of Jeremiah ever made.

WHAT THIS MEANS FOR US

First, no empire lasts forever. Babylon seemed invincible. It fell. Rome seemed eternal. It fell. Every human power structure that sets itself up as ultimate and permanent will eventually collapse. Only the kingdom of God endures. When the powers of this world seem overwhelming, remember that God has outlasted every empire that has ever existed, and he will outlast whatever comes next.

Second, God holds all nations accountable, not just his own people. The oracles against the nations make it clear that violence, arrogance, and injustice are not tolerated anywhere. God's moral standards are universal. No nation gets a free pass just because it's powerful or because God used it for a season.

Third, God grieves over the suffering of people who aren't his covenant people. He wept for Moab. He lamented over Damascus. The God of the Bible is not a tribal deity who only cares about one group. His compassion extends to the whole world, even to nations under his judgment. If God's heart breaks for people who don't know him, ours should too.

Fourth, hope doesn't have to be dramatic to be real. The book ends with a quiet scene in a Babylonian court, an old king getting better food and a better seat. No fireworks. No armies marching home. Just a small, steady sign that God's promises were still alive. Sometimes hope looks like a prison door opening. Sometimes it looks like kindness in an unexpected place. Don't miss the small signs of grace just because they don't look the way you expected.

Fifth, the story isn't over. The book of Jeremiah ends, but the story it tells keeps going. The new covenant Jeremiah promised would be sealed in the blood of Jesus at the Last Supper. The righteous Branch he prophesied would be born in a stable and crowned on a cross. The restoration he envisioned would extend not just to Israel but to every nation, tribe, and language on earth. Jeremiah saw the beginning of something he wouldn't live to see completed. We live in the middle of that same story, still waiting for its final chapter.

TALKING POINTS

1. **God's oracles addressed nations all across the ancient world.** What does it mean that the God of Israel claims authority over nations that don't worship him? How does that shape the way you think about God's relationship to the whole world, not just to people who believe in him?

2. **God wept over Moab, a nation that had been Israel's enemy for centuries.** What does it tell you about God's character that he grieves over the suffering of nations under his own judgment? How should that affect the way we think about people we consider enemies or outsiders?

3. **Babylon was used by God as an instrument of judgment but was then judged for its own sins.** What does that teach about the difference between being used by God and being approved by God? Can you think of modern examples where something served a purpose for a time but shouldn't be treated as permanently good?

4. **The book ends with Jehoiachin being released from prison, a small and quiet act of grace after hundreds of pages of judgment.** Why do you think the editors chose to end the book this way? What does it say about how God works that the final note is not a thundering conclusion but a whisper of kindness?

5. **Jeremiah never saw most of his prophecies fulfilled. He died in Egypt, far from the land he loved, among people who refused to listen. Yet his words are still being read**

thousands of years later. What does his life teach about faithfulness when you can't see the results? How do you keep going when you can't see the ending?

The book of Jeremiah is finished. But the prophet's voice still echoes.

It echoes in every generation that wrestles with the gap between what God demands and what his people deliver. It echoes in every person who has ever felt called to speak a truth that nobody wants to hear. It echoes in every broken heart that dares to believe that God's plans for hope and a future might actually be true.

Jeremiah wept for his people. God wept through him. And then God made a promise: a new covenant, written not on stone but on the human heart. A relationship with God that no failure could destroy, because it would be held together not by our faithfulness but by his.

That promise found its answer in Jesus. And because it did, the last word of this ancient book is not judgment. It is not exile. It is not silence.

It is grace.